I0748214

More Aster(ix) Anthologies

Bending
Spring 2024

10th Anniversary Issue, Part II: Fiction & Interviews
Fall/Winter 2023

10th Anniversary Issue, Part I: Poetry & Nonfiction
Spring/Summer 2023

The Tarot Issue
December 2022

Mothers Unearthed
September 2022

Winter Fiction
December 2021

Best of Hot Metal Bridge
April 2021

The Ferrante Project
October 2020

The Poetry Issue
Winter 2020

Inheritance
Summer 2019

(Un)bound [double issue]
Winter 2018/2019

and more!
available for order wherever books are sold

Aster(ix) Journal

www.asterixjournal.com

Aster(ix) print issues are usually published 2 times a year in print with additional content online. **Aster(ix)** is funded in part by the Dietrich School of Arts and Sciences and the Department of English at University of Pittsburgh.

Aster(ix) Journal

presents

Longing

* * *

Edited by
Tanya Shirazi-Galvez

with
Adriana E. Ramírez

December 2024

BLUE SKETCH PRESS | PITTSBURGH

Published via Blue Sketch Press, Pittsburgh.
www.bluesketchpress.com

Longing: December 2024
An Aster(ix) Anthology / Aster(ix) Journal
Edited by Tanya Shirazi-Galvez with Adriana E. Ramírez—1st ed.

ISBN (print) 978-1-942547-23-5 (trade paperback)
1-942547-23-5 (ISBN-10)

Cover art by Iliana Emilia García
Cover Design by Little Owl Creative

First Edition: December 2024

Printed in the United States of America
9 8 7 6 5 4 3 2 1

Soy ese silencio que habita en nosotros,
que aspira en su espera poder expresar
tantas cosas muy simples a amigos y otros
que entiendan mi voz que es tan solo mirar.

— Gabriel Barrella Rosa

Contents

A Note from the Editor

Tanya Shirazi-Galvez

"My library is an archive of longings."
— Susan Sontag

Longing is inextricable from desire, pain, grief. We can long to return to a past, one where our fears, preoccupations, sorrows feel opaque in comparison to the joy, love and ecstasy that make our lives feel whole. The desire for what we cannot have. Or for what never was, never existed. For the unfinished, the undone, a pause in the past.

In these works, we long for the opportunity to see the graduation caps that never went up in the air, a yearning to be loved again, we "remember the blood." A response to a job opportunity has catastrophic consequences for a budding flower shop, a community is marked after an unspeakable crime, a widow finds freedom in unexpected ways, a daughter experiences inexplicable pain. We reexamine childhood memories that have instilled shame and revisit mother tongues.

The included conversations explore what can be salvaged from the drafting graveyard, how ghosts and ancestors are called on to write collaboratively, creating a "diasporic documentary," how family documents can be portals for aspects of oneself and a family narrative.

As this year comes to a close, while we wait, we here at Aster(ix) invite you to build an archive of longing with us.

With warmth,

Tanya

Teaching Myself Translation

Catalina Bode

I am teaching myself translation. Not to translate, but to better understand what it means to live between languages. To live inside and outside of them. It is my latest obsession.

I was born in the Netherlands to a Colombian mother and a German father. I grew up in Spanish, English, German, and Dutch—I lost the latter when we moved from the Netherlands to the States. When a writer I meet tells me the prophetic calling of her first word, book, I marvel at this origin story, then wonder, in what language did I first speak?

Spanish is my mother tongue and my mother's tongue. When asked if I am fluent in Spanish, I answer, fluency is a spectrum. This is true, but what I mean to say is that I can live a life in Spanish: I can open a bank account and rent an apartment and go on long walks in the mountains with a friend, but I probably read at the fourth grade level; I tremble and trip and lose all my words when I am nervous; I forget realizar does not mean to realize. I can live a life in Spanish, yes, but I cannot live my English life in Spanish.

* * *

As an undergrad, I fell in love with Jhumpa Lahiri; I fell in love with nostalgia and exile and questions of belonging. Lahiri, born in London to Indian immigrants, moved to Rhode Island at the age of three. She grew up watching her parents mourn their language, Bengali. This was before the instant-ness of the internet, before we could so easily reach and retrace, a time when her parents gripped onto letters in their language, reread what their beloveds had said again and again for a flicker of proximity. It is complicated, Lahiri's relationship to Bengali. It is a language she cannot read or write in. A language that, despite trying all her girlhood, she cannot speak without a foreign accent. She wanted to be both *completely [her parents'] daughter* and *considered an American*, but could be neither. Bengali, Lahiri explains, is both her mother tongue and a foreign tongue.

In *Beyond the Mother Tongue*, Yasemin Yildiz explores how the monolingual paradigm shapes the discourse on multilingualism, where 'mother tongue' creates constraint. She argues:

> The "mother tongue" functions as a shorthand that barely need explication. In this shorthand, the weight of the argument falls on the element of "mother" in Muttersprache. It stands for a unique, irreplaceable, unchangeable biological origin that situates the individual automatically in a kinship network and by extension in the nation.

Later, she writes:

> The notion of the unique "mother" insists on one predetermined and socially sanctioned language as the single locus of affect and attachment and thus attempts to obscure the possibility that languages other than the first or even

primary one can take on emotional meaning.

How does our relationship to language change when we think beyond its ties to ethnicity and nationality?

For this, I am fascinated by Jhumpa Lahiri's move into Italian—a language she studied for many years 'in exile', away from its roots, before moving to Rome. Of her voyage across the Atlantic, Lahiri writes: *it will be the first true departure of my life.* I wonder if she would also call it a departure *from* her life. A move that marks a previous life, and a new one.

There is a tenderness in the way she writes about Italian: *It's like a person met one day by chance, with whom I immediately feel a connection, of whom I feel fond.* She is in love, she says, it is a doting relationship, one of magical intimacy—yet it is unrequited. *The language will never need me.*

Need catches me. Can language *need* us? Is it not people, place, and circumstance that gives language need? Or can we offer a new language something it needs? Can we give it translations?

* * *

As I walk across campus with my new librarian friend, I tell her about my latest reading—a study on the varying translations of Wang Wei's "Deer Park". Eliot Weinberger describes two kinds of Chinese translators: *there are scholars: most are incapable of writing poetry, but a few can… And there are poets: most know no Chinese, a few some.* I mention my horror at approaching a translation of a poem I couldn't read, but

Weinberger observes how translations by poets, rather than scholars, better understand the poem. My friend offers another framework: in the world of library science, this is a question of *accuracy* and *aboutness*. The poets, she says, may be better at approaching aboutness.

I am interested in the phrase 'approaching aboutness'. Not arrival, not delivery, but nearing.

Kate Briggs, in *A Little Art*, captures this nearing:

> We need translations, urgently: it is through translation that we are able to reach the literatures written in the languages we don't or can't read, from the places where we don't or can't live, offering us a chance of understanding as well as the necessary and instructive experience of failing to understand them, of being confused and challenged by them.

We are reaching, trying, and failing at a chance of understanding.

* * *

There are Spanish words I did not know existed in English. Caspa. Lunar. There are Spanish words that do not exist in English: Estrenar, Sobremesa, Tutear. For so long I thought caspa was a condition only my sisters and I, and the other kids at the Mexican grocery store, suffered from. Our Head & Shoulders commercials came in Spanish. The models always had brown hair and skin. They promised us no more salty scalps. Teased us with luscious long hair. In high school I learned others knew of this thing that flaked from our heads. Dandruff! Dandruff! Dandruff! The thrill of finding a new word, as ugly as it might be.

Lunar has a translation, but I have always hated the word mole. Mole, for me, carried stigma. It is an unearthed rodent. A thing that comes with stray long hairs and requires surgical removal. Not lunares, no, my sisters and I made constellations of the brown dots along our body. My mother poked my sister's back, *Did you know your tío Vicente has one right there? And your tía Ana too. And right here,* she'd press into our skin, *your Abuelo had one, too.* Our lunares carried our lineage. We wanted to know whose little moons we had inherited.

* * *

In an interview with Paul Holdengräber, Jhumpa Lahiri recalls a wallet she gifted her mother. Inside the wallet's photo pocket, Lahiri slipped a picture of the building in Kolkata where her mother grew up. This place, Lahiri describes, was her mother's Ithaca, *her everything, the place where she was happy.* It is also the place Lahiri has always stood outside of. Her parent's language, their home, a planet she mooned. Preserved behind a thin piece of plastic film, Lahiri gifted her mother a pocket homage to the center of her mother's happiness. Imagine, to reach into your pocket and touch plastic, and not the cement and dust of home. A haunting proximity.

In a letter to Fawwaz Traboulsi, Etel Adnan writes of chasing her mother's voice: *I went to Greece hoping to hear the Greek spoken by my mother. I listened closely, and it seemed that no one spoke the way she did.*

I chase my mother's Spanish too. I have lost her and fear losing the language that celebrated my first wobbly steps. I catch it rarely, the mountain sounds of my mother's Colombia. My monthly calls with her sister, my aunt, are not enough. We are all retracing our mothers—

the piece of them we cannot have; a home we cannot belong to.

For a year I lived in Asturias, Spain, to meet my Spanish self. Of course, no one there spoke the way she did. I found it disorienting, at first, to live in the Europe of my father, but in the language of my mother. But then, it became a place that was untethered to them. My mountain and my cows and my café con leche. Not *my* as in ownership or as in belonging to me, but *my* as in denoting relation, a friendship perhaps, one that felt so separate from my parents.

* * *

At the age of four, I moved from the Netherlands to the cornfields of Illinois. I lost my Dutch soon after, but for a period of my childhood, I forgot that I ever knew the language. I told my father of the made-up language I spoke in daycare, amazed how despite speaking in gibberish, my friend and I understood each other completely.

Dutch, my father said, *you were speaking Dutch.*

In memory, I had made the language alien.

My father woke my sisters and I every Sunday morning with his German. His voice, the only bridge across the Atlantic. I learned to sleep through shouted German. And while I tried many times, I have never learned the language. At eleven, I figured out how to say my age. Ich bin elf jahre alt. I was eleven for many years. In grad school, I audited half a semester of German until I grew embarrassed to be so much slower than the eighteen year-olds who had also studied the language in high school. A shame.

Ich bin sechsundzwanzig jahre alt. I am twenty-six years old.

Ich bin Kolumbianerin. Ich bin Deutsche. Ich studiere Literatur.

I don't feel towards German what I feel towards Spanish. There's no grief wrapped up in it. There is something about the disappearing of the mother tongue when you live outside of it—a unique distance that no other language acquisition can know. This grief is the emotional attachment I think we talk about when we talk about our first language(s).

* * *

When I visit my father's house, I find the baby book my mother made where she documented my first word: Quac Quac. She writes it half in Spanish, half English.

Quack
    Cuac

Perhaps my first language is bird. A language of flight, of migration. An in-between. A translation.

* * *

Kate Briggs thoughtfully imagines translation as 'a table' and 'to table', as in *to submit for consideration, to propose, as well as to suspend consideration indefinitely*. It is also, etymologically, *a plate, a meal, an offering*. Or alternatively, *the thinking itself and the configuration of persons and relations around it.*

It is a commitment to togetherness, to uncertainty, to relation and limbo at once.

In Jessica Gaitán Johannesson's debut novel, *How We are Translated*, a Swedish woman named Kristin contemplates her pregnancy while working at a museum in Edinburgh, where she role-plays as a Viking. While working, Kristin is only permitted to speak in Swedish. Before each shift she must spend twenty minutes in the 'Translation Room', where the actors must *leave [their] English-speaking everydays tidily outside*, and return to their native language. The Translation Room's intended function is a place of meditation and renunciation, but our narrator is incapable of tidy abandon. Her English and Swedish cannot be compartmentalized into two lives. She is always living in the Translation Room.

In murky preparation for the potential baby, Kristin's partner begins to learn Swedish. Kristin presses to know more about his childhood. Adopted by a Scottish family at a young age, he remembers little from his life in Brazil. She asks about the voyage, about his adopted mother. *You get on the plane, and then you get off, and at some point she becomes ma*, she says. She is getting at a question of intimacy: when did you call that woman who picked you up in the airport, Mom? How does someone else become your mother? Or what Johannesson is really asking, how do we relate to our adopted tongues? Who does language tie us to?

* * *

Our estrangement to our first language(s) shapes our relationship to language itself. It is a ghost tongue in the cave of our mouths. *Bengali will be taken away when my parents are no longer here*, Lahiri writes. It is the language that formed her relationship to language—one of linguistic exile. It is what she admires of Italo Calvino, his ability to straddle *places and languages...acutely aware of what could be mined from a detachment from one's own origins.* Italian is Lahiri's bridge to another planet, a moon tugged elsewhere. It offers Lahiri a new way of being inside and outside of something, the way she has always looked at language, a new margin to make home.

Works Referenced

Adnan, Etel. *Of Cities & Women: Letters to Fawwaz.* Post-Apollo Press, 1993.

Briggs, Kate. *This Little Art.* Fitzcarraldo Editions, 2021.

Holdengräber, Paul, and Jhumpa Lahiri. *"My Mother's Nostalgia." Youtube.com,* New York Public Library, 4 Mar. 2016.

Johannesson, Jessica Gaitan. *How We Are Translated.* Scribe, 2022.

Lahiri, Jhumpa. *Translating Myself and Others.* Princeton University Press, 2022.

Lahiri, Jhumpa, and Ann Goldstein. *In Other Words.* Bloomsbury, 2017.

Weinberger, Eliot, and Octavio Paz. *19 Ways of Looking at Wang Wei: With More Ways.* New Directions Books, 2016.

Yildiz, Yasemin. *Beyond the Mother Tongue: The Postmonolingual Condition.* Fordham Univ. Press, 2014.

Flower Shop

Tierney Oberhammer

Five

The 300-balloon arch is twenty-five feet long, a candy-colored display of peach, gold, and Tiffany Blue curving over the brunch spread. Plates of French toast, eggs Benedict, and shakshuka crowd a cream tablecloth. Candles drip. Guests pick at their food. The wait staff alternates between refilling coffee cups and passing out mimosas and bloody Marys. Lena is not drinking because she is pregnant, but she encourages her friends to have fun. It's her baby shower. She orders another bottle of champagne and relishes in the attention her round belly brings her. She'd never been popular in school, and she likes the taste of it.

In the middle of the table, a white ceramic vase holds a single pink flower. Lena recognizes it. The carnation is the cheapest flower, she thinks, but it is not the least beautiful. She'd often confused certain rose varieties with carnations when she helped Ana at the shop. The flowers were that similar. But the rainbow carnations that Ana dyed were ugly. Ana had been tacky. Ana *liked* doing the floral arrangements for Sweet Sixteens. Ana had lacked class. She lacked manners, too.

The baby twitches inside Lena's womb like a fish flicking its tail, and Lena returns her attention to the party. She is reminded so often of the flower shop that she resents Ana for hiring her in the first place. The memories are an unwanted distraction. How many baby showers will be thrown in her honor? She must soak up the experience. Scheduled sex hadn't been pleasant.

Lena's mother sits across the table from Lena shining with pride. Her eyes have been misty all morning. The first child of her only daughter! Packages wrapped in every shade of yellow topple over one another on the gift counter. The food is rich and plentiful, and the space is light-filled. Still, an image of Ana flits through Lena's mind. Small, brown-skinned, and stony-faced.

Last week, when Lena had dropped by the shop one afternoon to make sure Ana understood the lawyer's letter, Ana wouldn't even look at Lena.

"You probably feel confused," Lena had said, taking a step toward her. "And I'm genuinely sorry it has to be this way."

Ana had stepped back behind the counter, and Lena suddenly felt aware of her body, of the room. She was large, looming, and the smell of plant life was thick. Had her visit to the shop been an overstep? Lena had been the shop assistant for close to a year. How could Ana, a working mother of two, not see that firing Lena for being pregnant had been unethical? And then rebuke the olive branch Lena offered by stopping by? Couldn't they have both expressed regret for the way things had turned out? Island cultures were supposed to value community. Lena might have dropped the whole thing, had Ana had more grace.

At least Lena had learned something through the flower shop ordeal. Recently, she'd added a floral consultation to the end of a client meeting. It was her first paid project as an interior designer in years. "Carnations are underrated," she'd said to the friend of her mother, who needed a quote for a living room refresh. It was a simple statement—"carnations are underrated"—but it worked. It helped Lena communicate that she was of the people. Not uppity, like so many of her peers.

Lena has an $80,000 Steinway baby grand on the first floor of her house. "It's a rental," she assures friends, talking about the piano. "I keep meaning to play, but then I'm so busy with work." Her Brooklyn brownstone, on the other hand, is not a rental. "It has good bones," Lena told her father over mezcal margaritas during a long weekend in San Miguel the previous year. "The neighborhood is up-and-coming." The domestic mineral business had brought Lena's father surprising wealth. He had already put Lena through art school, and if Lena was going to be an interior designer, she needed interiors to design. So the house was hers. "An early wedding present," he had said, footing the half-a-million down payment.

Lena picks up her phone to check Zillow. After a year, Brooklyn has lost its shine. Lately she's been thinking about her brownstone as an investment property. A little design project. Something to flip and make extra money from. There's no parking in Bed-Stuy, and the nearest garage is six blocks away. It's loud, too. Every afternoon, Lena hears kids from the nearby high school shouting as class lets out. Plus, with the baby coming, maybe it's time to leave the city. Lena is not twenty-five anymore.

She sees a listing for a gorgeous 1929 Tudor home on a half-acre in Larchmont, just forty-five minutes north of the city. It sits on a small hill, and the lawn is a brilliant green thanks to an underground sprinkler system. A high-end renovation features French doors, hardwood flooring and a restored fireplace. Lena takes a screenshot of the listing and sends it to her father. Chances are he'll know an agent showing the property. She wonders if the piano rental company that she uses delivers to Westchester. Maybe with the extra time and space, she'll finally start music lessons.

"Hey!" Lena's sister-in-law claps her hands together on the other side of the table. "I have some advice for our mother-to-be."

"Don't get a Jamaican nanny," interrupts a friend from art school. "I know how it sounds. But trust me."

The sister-in-law frowns, then rolls her eyes. "Two words," she says. "Night nurse. I wouldn't have survived without one."

Lena's mother wants to know what a night nurse is.

"God's gift to working mothers. They stay overnight to feed and change the baby so you can sleep."

"Sounds expensive."

"Send me her contact information," Lena says. Such synchronicity, she thinks. She can put her settlement money toward a night nurse. It's perfect, but she keeps it to herself. Lena hasn't told any of her friends about the lawsuit. She barely told her fiancé. None of them would have understood.

Even her lawyer, a trained steward of ethics, had used the word "sue" while discussing the case over the phone. "You want to sue?" she'd said, incredulously. Lena didn't like her choice of words and had paused, collected herself, and worked to clarify.

"It's symbolic, of course. It's not about money. It's the principle."

The lawyer coughed, then excused herself. "Of course. I'll start drafting a demand letter." Lena had felt self-conscious then, too. Still, it was more than obvious that she was the wronged party.

Lena was somewhat familiar with the legal process. Her senior year of college, she hired someone to write a paper for her, and the adjunct professor caught on. My *tutor* and I worked on the paper *together*, Lena explained to the department head, and then the chancellor. She had hired a *tutor*. The professor was unaware that Lena's father had made significant donations to the college since Lena's enrollment. At his daughter's urging, Mr. Hartman had accused the adjunct professor of defamation, and her contract with the school lapsed at the end of the semester. For that, Lena had felt bad. She had been cheating. Enough time had passed that she could admit the truth. It had been excessive for her school to threaten expulsion over the misstep, yes, but the teacher needn't have suffered. But Lena had been young at the time, self-centered. Now she was embarrassed about the way it had gone down. The privilege she'd wielded. This time was different, though. In her heart, Lena knew that she was standing up for women and mothers everywhere. But she didn't want to have to explain, so she told people she quit. Everyone had said, "Makes sense."

There was right, and there was wrong. Pregnancy discrimination was wrong.

Four

The FedEx envelope is addressed to *Ms. Ana Gomez*, and it arrives at the flower shop a month after Lena's last day, the day she'd stormed out red-faced. Ana's new employee, a hard-working high school senior, signs for the envelope, then hands it to Ana as he leaves to run deliveries. Later Ana, her husband David, and their girls will sit together and have dinner. For now, Rosa and Lily watch cartoons and giggle in the back room while Ana luxuriates in the peace their new iPad grants her. Working on a flower arrangement for the next morning, Ana holds baby blue eucalyptus against a bin of orange roses to gauge the color palette.

Ana is designing a wedding bouquet that is inspired by a "New York sunset"—the bride's words, not hers—but she likes the concept. Engrossed, she puts the FedEx envelope next to the cash register. The client is on a budget, but Ana is determined that nobody will suspect it based on the flower arrangements. Lavender carnations, pink lilies, and a few creamsicle-colored roses, all nestled among silver-gray lamb's ear. The arrangement is carnation-heavy, but they work to spotlight the more expensive flowers, which are like the glowing edges of a cloud that fails to obscure the sun. She starts to plan how she will stage the bouquet for social media. The shop's following is growing; she just hit the 2,000 mark. People seem to like the photos of her children the most.

When Ana tears open the letter, it is the end of the day and she is tired. The letter is long and serious with formal headings. She skims its contents and her eyes land on "loyal employee," "wrongfully," "undue hardship," and "discrimination." There is a number, $10,000, buried in the last paragraph. Concerned, Ana returns to the first page and examines the sender. It's an unfamiliar address. Then she reads the opening paragraph and sees Lena's name.

"On behalf of Lena Hartman," the letter says. Though Ana is unfamiliar with the Equal Employment Opportunity Commission, she understands that Lena Hartman is threatening her. As she reads the details of the letter more carefully, and shows the letter to David that night, she understands that it was a mistake to fire Lena. No, it was a mistake to hire Lena.

Ana asks friends if anyone has a lawyer to recommend, and someone puts her in touch with the cousin of a colleague's wife. Frustratingly, the immigration lawyer Ana speaks with is more concerned with David's green card status entering the equation than anything related to pregnancy discrimination. When the lawyer googles "Hartman," she lowers her tone and asks Ana if she has the money.

Three

When Ana tapes up a help wanted sign, Lena Hartman, the lonely housewife, is the last person she expects to hire. She imagines a teenager from the high school on Marcy will come on the weekends. A student athlete maybe, since there are heavy boxes to lift. She and David are prepared to offer $10 an hour, cash, and only fifteen hours each week. But Lena is pushy about wanting the job.

David warms quickly to the idea of a rich, white lady dealing with customers, while Ana wants to stick with the original plan to hire a kid.

"You're not the one who's going to have to talk to her," she says.

"But she knows things," David argues.

Ana sucks her teeth. "What things?"

She ignores David all through dinner, focusing on the girls, the radio, anything but him. Later, in bed, she agrees that more people like Lena coming to the shop isn't a bad thing.

"Let's just see," David says.

The work is not hard, Ana thinks. They can give this woman something to do. When she agrees to hire Lena, it is more out of pity than anything else.

On Lena's days, Ana hands her a list of addresses and a trunk full of flowers. Lena returns hours later, tired but spirited, often with an iced latte and a bagged pastry. Doing deliveries is gratifying, Ana knows. She can see it on Lena's face, and Lena says so, too. "It is a gift to give," she remarks. The women agree that even grieving customers light up when armfuls of white lilies or funeral roses arrive.

Ana imagines that Lena's job is made even more enjoyable because she has a shiny black SUV to drive around in. Unlike David in the rusted-out van, Lena never returns looking overwhelmed. She remains unaware of the rising rent, the bookkeeping, the money Ana and David send home to both of their parents. Lena asks multiple times a week what Ana is doing at the computer.

"Money," Ana says. "I'm doing the money."

Though it is innocent, curious, Lena's question annoys Ana. What does she think a business is? Lena reminds Ana of a kid making a game out of work.

"Let's play flower shop!" she's heard her own children say, equipped with flower clippings and a few nickels. Then, "Let's play wedding!"

Play education, play doctor, play lawyer, Ana wants to tell them.

Often, Lena arrives late and leaves early. After her deliveries, she chats with customers, recommending first flowers, and then retinol creams and yoga studios and upstate vacation properties. Ana does the math and calculates that every week Lena spends most of her paycheck on pastries and to-go coffees. The rest she spends on flowers. But the customers return, and most of the time they buy what Lena recommends. Lena's book club comes into the shop, and Lena gives them a tour of the different sections, and then brings them to the register to buy hundreds of dollars worth of flowers.

"Let me ring you up," Lena says. The women pay with credit cards, and Lena adds a 5% service charge without asking. After the group leaves, Lena turns to Ana to explain. "Was that OK? It's kind of standard. I think it's a good idea."

Ana laughs, waves Lena away. "Yes, sure. A great idea."

On a Thursday, Lena returns from her deliveries earlier than usual. An old man in a waxed jacket and loafers enters the store in front of her. His patterned button-down hangs loose on a lanky frame, and the bright spot on his bald head shines as he looks around. His skin is tanned.

"This is my father," Lena announces, and the man smiles.

They don't match, Ana thinks, looking back and forth between father and daughter. Lena has sharp lines on a soft body, a round face with penciled eyebrows and a blunt haircut framing the beginning of a double chin. Her father is thin and well-postured. "Congratulations," he says, grinning at the bins of roses displayed at the front of the store. "It's a pleasure to meet you." His blue eyes sparkle. For a moment, Ana is unsure why he is congratulating her. But as she watches him breathe in the sweet smell of the shop, she catches herself smiling. Who knows what nonsense Lena told him. He seems friendly. He is filled with wonder. "Nice to meet you," Ana says. He chuckles. "I hope my daughter isn't giving you any grief."

"Ha ha," Lena says, rolling her eyes. She steps closer to Ana, leaving her father to admire the sunflowers. "My dad wants to take me for a coffee." She smiles, already backing away from the counter. "I'll bring you something. What kind of muffin do you like?"

Ana looks around the shop. It has been a slow morning, and everything is in its place. "Nothing for me." she says. "But maybe something for the girls?" Rosa and Lily have been playing quietly in the storeroom since lunchtime, and she doesn't expect it to last much longer. "Of course," Lena says.

Lena's father approaches the register with a bundle of sunflowers. "For Lena's mother. Happy wife, happy life." He winks, pays, and they walk out together, Lena leading the way. When she returns twenty-five minutes later, Lena is alone. She sets a box of muffins on the counter and hands Ana a to-go cup. "Milk and sugar," she says, which is exactly how Ana likes her coffee. Ana makes a mental note to apologize to

David later. Maybe he'd been right about Lena. She isn't that bad. The father is nice. Funny.

After a few uneventful months, Lena announces she is pregnant. She tears up as she delivers the news, and Ana recalls the feeling of being with child. As miraculous as it was mundane, to be making life.

"I can't lift anything more than thirty-five pounds. And I can't stand for long periods." Lena touches her belly. "But I can answer the phone."

Ana and David need Lena to lift heavy boxes, though. They need her to drive across town with ten centerpieces, dropping them at ten different addresses. Ana thinks maybe Lena can watch Rosa and Lily while she manages things up front, but soon Rosa is crying and Lena is saying that she can't carry the girls around. "How much do they weigh?" Lena asks and points out that she isn't a babysitter, anyway.

Ana tries to remember being pregnant for the first time. The worry and uncertainty. But the work starts to pile up all the same. Soon, Ana and David are staying late again, finishing the day's tasks. Rosa and Lily are overtired and have meltdowns at bedtime. Exactly what they were trying to avoid when they'd hired Lena. "I worked through two babies," Ana says to David. "We can't pay her if she can't do the job." David agrees that they need to talk to Lena.

Two

Double-bolting her front entry, Lena Hartman is aware that she and her fiancé are two of very few white, non-native New Yorkers on her new block. But gentrification is tricky! And Bed-Stuy is an affordable, up-and-coming neighborhood. A whole building for the cost of a Manhattan apartment. Five bedrooms, four baths. A back patio and a half-finished basement. She is tearing out all the ugly pine cabinetry in the kitchen and replacing it with high-gloss white lacquer touch cabinets. Subway tiles for the backsplash. A marble counter. Oak floors stained gray, and, of course, all new appliances. The bathrooms she plans to do in the style of her favorite boutique hotel. Simple. Understated. Cement and frosted glass. And everything else just needs a fresh coat of paint. The brownstone still has its original molding—that is a blessing—and since she has given up a doorman in favor of a whole townhouse, she plans to install a security system with a video intercom.

On Fridays, Lena starts visiting the family-owned flower shop down the block to purchase fresh bouquets for her living room and kitchen. Even in the midst of the renovations, cut flowers make the house a home. Plus, she feels part of the community when she pushes the glass door into the quaint little shop. The displays at the flower shop are not the Martha Stewart–quality she was accustomed to in Manhattan, but they eclipse the options in her Wisconsin hometown, which were more bunched than arranged. The shop's walls are pink and green, and fairy lights dot the ceiling. She lets the owners design whatever bouquet they want. "I trust you," she says, maintaining eye contact. After months of regular visits, she considers Ana, the wife, and David, the husband, friends. Real friends. Or at least close acquaintances.

Sure, there's a minor communication barrier, but Lena studied abroad in Spain her junior year. She can tell it delights Ana and David when she speaks to them in Spanish. "¿Cómo están las niñas?" she says, asking about little Rosa and Lily, who are probably in the back watching TV. She tells her art school friends about the time she spends at the shop with Ana, David, and their two young girls. She feels good about the money she spends there, her little investment in the community. When she sees a sign in the storefront window, "We Are Hiring," it occurs to Lena that she could apply. Why not, she thinks, do more? It would be unconventional, sure. But it was interesting. Experiential. And she desperately needs something to do.

At first, Ana Gomez laughs. "You want to work here?" she says, raising her eyebrows. Lena feels impatient as she watches Ana bend to lift a box onto her workstation. She takes scissors to the top of it and starts stacking its contents onto a nearby shelf. "I've always wanted to learn about the business," Lena replies. She watches Ana strain to lift a second box onto the table. It contains small plastic bags filled with tiny, polished pebbles. "It's not a job for you," Ana says.

For this, Lena resents Ana. What does Ana know of Lena, of her capabilities and potential for contribution? What does Ana know of anything? Ana's hiring efforts amount to a paper "Help Wanted" sign taped to a dirty window. Lena feels judged. But just a fingernail's scratch beneath her indignation, she knows that she's never had a job, not really. The summer after her senior year, her mother's best friend presented her with an internship at an architecture firm. She wasn't an architect, so her tasks had been limited. Research, file management, social media. But after three months, she felt certain she could take what she'd learned, combine it with her fine arts education, and launch a home renovation business. She just needed her father's credit card to pay for the business website.

On the day of its launch, Lena threw a party to celebrate the inauguration of her #girlboss life. Her classmates spoke loudly as they passive-aggressively critiqued late-stage capitalism. Her then-boyfriend rolled his eyes, but even he did not come to her defense. Now, several years later, her secret shame is that the most effort she ever put into her business had been the website and launch party. Good ideas came easily to her, but momentum wasn't her strong suit. And so, this job at the flower shop was a chance to prove herself.

At home, on the phone, Lena whines to her father about Ana and David. "I could bring them a lot of new clients. They have no online presence." She pours a glass of red wine and drops an ice cube into it. "Honestly," she takes a sip. "I could make a difference."

"Mmm," her father agrees. "You know what they say about idle hands."

The next day, Lena returns to Ana with the promise that she will send all of her friends to the flower shop. "And then you'll get referrals from those people," she says. Ana stops rummaging around in the supply closet and nods. She's listening. Lena can tell she is considering it now. After all, Ana is a businesswoman.

Late morning on the third day, chimes jingle as Lena pushes into the flower shop. She breathes in the familiar scent of rose, lilac, and greenery. Ana and David are in the back talking. Lena rarely sees them in the shop at the same time and takes it as a good sign. Lena smiles wide. Ana glances at her husband, then nods. She turns to Lena. "OK," she says. "We can try."

Lena squeals and rushes over to hug Ana. "You won't regret this," she says.

And so, on Thursday, Friday, and Saturday afternoons, Lena does deliveries and helps Ana close up. She rearranges arrangements and sweeps the tiled floor. She learns how to run the register. She feels accomplished and is proud of the slim envelope of twenties Ana hands her at the end of the week. The job is clearly good for her. She rarely goes for a second glass of wine in the evenings anymore, and she falls asleep easily. When Rosa or Lily want to be held, Lena lifts them up and hugs them as if they were her own.

One

Ana Gomez fries eggs for dinner in her family's one-bedroom apartment fourteen blocks from their store. She lays out bread and butter. Her children like American cheese, so she puts it out, too. Tomorrow she will prepare vegetables and meat. It's not that they can't afford it. It's just that it's past nine o'clock, and Rosa and Lily need to get to bed. It's summer, and they are with Ana all day, every day, driving her crazy. They want snacks. A puzzle piece has fallen out of reach. One of them has pinched the other.

Ana's husband, David, is asleep already because tomorrow at four a.m. he will leave their apartment in Brooklyn and drive their junky Nissan to 28th Street to pick up roses, lilies, orchids, hydrangea, tulips, and peonies, along with greens and fillers. He's lucky, Ana thinks, to be in bed while Rosa whines that the ketchup is runny. Ana misses sitting in the passenger seat for early morning rides over the Manhattan Bridge and through a Chinatown so quiet it is unrecognizable. For David's sake, she prays the van doesn't overheat again.

Farther north, florists and set designers and restaurateurs double park between 6th and 7th Avenue to load their open trunks with flowers. August is for marigolds and sunflowers, and Ana would love to see the thick bands of orange and yellow in the warehouses. She wants to smell the grassy fragrance, clean and sharp. But she never learned how to drive back home—hadn't needed to—and so it is David's routine to make the trip to the city for the flowers. Before the girls, it was different.

For the past several years, Ana and David have spent every day at the shop, hours past close. Ana, packing and unpacking, caring for cut flowers and taking inventory. David, making deliveries, running errands, and doing maintenance. Their children fuss until they fall asleep in the back room. But business is good. These days, people want flowers for no reason. Nobody is getting married. Nobody died. Ten years ago, it was weddings, funerals, Valentine's Day, Mother's Day, and prom. Now, wealthy women call the shop to set up weekly deliveries. They pass by the store and pick something from the window display. "Flowers just really brighten a room," they say, too slowly. Ana is patient. She nods. She knows what money looks like. It is understated, in dark colors. It asks for the price when the price is already displayed. It wants ease. It wants to feel validated.

Ana remembers her customers' names and thanks God for their spending habits as she hands over fresh cut stems wrapped in white paper. She avoids plastic, not because she is particularly "green," but because she is cultivating an eco-friendly reputation. "Always nice to see you," Ana tells Natalie Whitestone, a wealthy New England expat married to the even-wealthier heir of a European fashion brand. Natalie pays in crisp hundred-dollar bills.

Ana invents stories about other regulars, like Kenn, who turns as blush as hydrangeas at checkout. Perhaps the bouquets aren't for his wife, Ana muses, but for a mistress. Or a mister. Or maybe Kenn only comes to the shop to spend a few moments with Ana herself. Does he pine for her as she rings him up? She is a little bit older, but her long hair is glossy, and her teeth are white.

And then there's the new neighbor, Lena Hartman, who lingers whenever she stops by the shop, practicing her broken Spanish. She is in her late twenties, Ana guesses, with dyed chestnut brown hair. It's the patronage of people like her, loyal customers with expendable income, new to the neighborhood, that spells out success for Ana and her family. Now Ana and David are able to save. Soon they will replace the eighteen-year-old van that David spends half his time repairing. Then they will start a college fund for their daughters. Money is less and less of a problem. It's time that they don't have enough of.

Case in point, it is past 9 pm, and Ana is just now getting dinner on the table. Her girls ought to be in bed already, but instead corn chips and television stave their hunger. Lena Hartman kept them all at the shop an hour after close with a request for two custom arrangements. At $79 each, it was worth it. Still, how does Lena not know what time they close? She has quickly become the most regular regular. Fretting over her reflection in the display cases. Constantly checking her phone.

Ana feels a prickle of irritation as she recalls Lena Hartman's needy, moneyed presence in the shop. Over-caffeinated, making every greeting exuberant. Her smooth, pale skin, dewy and unmoving, and the diamond engagement ring she wears flipped toward her palm. Does she want to show off the stone or not? Lena is proof that all the money in the world can't buy someone a sense of self.

Ana shrugs. Pours two glasses of milk. She is giving the woman too much thought. De todos ha de haber en el mundo, she says to herself. It takes all types. She calls her daughters to the table, then decides they can eat on the living room floor just this once. After dinner, she will count the day's money. She hasn't told David yet, but soon they will hit the mark. Ten thousand dollars saved toward a car. It makes her smile to think about delivering the good news. The road to success is long, but she walks it with her family, and daily she is surrounded with flowers.

Interview with Elaine Hsieh Chou

Sangi Lama & Sandra Lee

Sangi Lama (SL): Thank you again, Elaine, for all your time and effort, and for being willing to do this interview. We're very excited to chat with you. I would love to start with asking you what your writing process is like. How do you generate ideas, or get started?

Elaine Hsieh Chou (EHC): Thank you for having me. So happy to be here. So with ideas, they come at the most random times. I might be falling asleep, or walking, or sometimes I'll be watching something, or reading something, and it'll spark another idea. So the ideas—I never know what triggers them or where they come from, but I always write them down immediately. Even when I'm tired and don't want to look at that blinding phone screen at night, I'm like, 'oh, no, open the notes app.' Always write it down because even when you're like, 'that's such a good idea, I'll remember it'—no, you won't. And then once I have an idea, I just start building on it, I suppose in different ways. If the idea is a really strong voice, I try to figure out, okay, who's this person and why am I interested in them?

And sometimes, I feel like in the past I'd be a little more concept-driven. Like, a story that I need to rewrite a lot that I actually wrote during my MFA is about this Asian-American man who's a hardcore Republican—not a great guy, in terms of his beliefs and everything.

And he joins this softball team of all racist white people, but he still really wants to join.That's his people. It turns out to be a KKK chapter. So he becomes the first Asian man to join the KKK. And that was such a concept-driven theme. I struggled with it so much because I just liked the idea of it, but I didn't want to spend any time with the character.

I didn't want to go into his head. I think I finally figured out a compromise. But it took many years because it was a cool idea. I remember when I was thinking about it. I was angry. I can't remember what it was, but it was our community being anti-Black, supporting the cops, whatever.

But because it was just content, it took me so long to go in and figure it out. I was trying to then honor my resistance to it because I was like, why do I have to go into his head? Why do I have to listen to that advice? And now I'm hoping to write it almost like an interview expose, of awful people who have done awful things and interview them in jail or wherever they are.

Anyways, long-winded answer to say, sometimes it might happen that way, that it really takes me a long time to figure it out, and then other times I'll see really vivid scenes and I'm like, okay, so these scenes—I'll let them guide me. And I just start writing down random ideas. I'm like, okay maybe he has a daughter. What kind of job could she have? and I just try to brainstorm as freely as I can and to try out any possible idea and possibility, and in the end begin to pick through it.

I always have a document that's literally called "brainstorm" for a specific idea, and then after I've emptied my head, I can think of nothing else, I'll try to find the thread of where it should start. And I always try to play around with different beginnings for fiction, because I feel like the beginning tells you everything. Literally the first word, the first sentence is the voice of it, is the point of view, and I have to feel it so specifically and strongly, or else… I'm not going to know where to go, and I get lost. I was just saying yesterday that I don't know if I'm a planner or a pantser, and I say I'm more of a pantser, but I guess I do prepare a lot for just that first part. And then when I feel confident in it, I feel like I can be more loose. Now I can see sort of what happens and not be as strict.

Sandra Lee (SSL): Thank you so much for sharing your process with us. I'd also be curious to hear how you got to the writing life. I know you started off in a PhD program and I'm curious how you then went from a PhD to an MFA.

EHC: I mean, I think I was always a writer. This is such a common answer. It's so boring, but I journaled a lot as a kid, and I wrote a lot of poems, like really emo poems, so I was always writing. And I remember in sixth grade, we had to write a short story. It was an assignment, and I loved it, but it was just like, "oh, that's homework." I never really thought of it again, but I was always writing in some way. Then I got to undergrad, and I was an English major, but there was an emphasis in creative writing, and I was like, "oh, that sounds fun. I'll take it and, and see what happens." I loved it.

The stuff I was writing—I didn't know what I was doing, because I didn't know who I was. And so I kept trying to mimic the authors we were reading. I didn't know what stories I needed to tell. All I knew was I loved this magic trick that I can make fake things seem real and make people feel things. It's fake, but what they feel is real. I was having a great time, definitely not writing the type of stuff I should have been writing, and then towards the end of my undergrad, I was like, okay, I have to find a career.

I didn't even think of creative writing. It was so divorced from what I thought a job was. And the funny thing is, our teachers were professors, and at no point did I ever really ask them. Maybe because they were professors, I ended up choosing academia. But at no point did I ask, "how did you become a writer?" I didn't even entertain that thought. I guess my brain completely shut out and was just like, "oh, well, I like my English classes, maybe I'll become an English professor." So that was my journey for a long time.

I'll skip over everything that happened with a PhD, that's another long story. But when I decided to quit and was like, what am I going to do with my life? Part of why I left was also this confrontation with my mortality and thinking about what do I want to do if I were to die? It was very dramatic. It was like, do I want to die in this musty old basement researching dead white people?

And I was like, no. I could resoundingly say no. And instead I was like, well, what is the thing I would die doing that I would risk it for, and I thought back to writing. It was just this dormant desire inside me that was too frightening to ever entertain. But when I was pushed to this certain place in my life, I was like, "what am I waiting for?" I have one life.

I quit the PhD program and started working at Shakespeare and Company in Paris, so I was surrounded by books and authors. It was a great space for me to be and to start writing. I was reading all the time, and just experimenting—writing little things here and there. But I'm stuck here in France. I still don't really know what I'm doing, I don't really know how to become a writer. And the one thing I could find that seemed concrete was an MFA program. And I thought, I'll have a reason to go back to the US, I don't have to move back to my parents. I think this is what I should do, this could be my path back in. I applied and ended up going to NYU and that's really how I found my way back.

SL: You've mentioned that you recognize connections late in the writing or publishing process. I'm curious to know, how much do you see writing as being a really intuitive or instinctive process? In what ways do you think you cultivate that or really try to protect those intuitions?

EHC: I have talked about trying to find the feeling of being alone in the room again. It's funny when writers are actively querying or they're waiting. They have an agent and they're on submission and they're like "this is the worst time of my life, all I want is to be published." I was like that too once? But the thing I realized is I can never get back to what it felt like to be alone in the room. And by alone in the room, I mean you're writing with the belief and the sort of certainty that no one's ever going to read what you're writing.

So it's a sort of privacy and freedom? Whereas now... if I write something with the intention of a short story, in the back of my head, if I like it, I'm gonna try to publish it. And I will probably have a means to do that now.

I don't have this protective cloak of like, will anyone read this? I don't know, but I'm having a great time. I'm always trying to get back there.

I think protecting that instinct is so key. Something I do is when, like, zero drafting—pure, pulling something out of thin air—I can't have any distractions. I need to feel like I can disappear from the world. And I think it's harder and harder to do.

I think it is harder and harder to find that space. But I think writing, in terms of it being intuitive, I think all our first entry points into writing are intuitive. And then I think it depends, because revision you could call not intuitive. You could call maybe all zero drafts intuitive, or maybe they should be, because you have to turn off the critic inside yourself, the person who decides this is good or this is bad, whatever that actually means, and just shut it off. Let the faucet run.

But then in revision—is any of that intuitive? Revision you have to sort of step away and dissect and look at it from ways that maybe aren't intuitive, which is why there are so many books and tips and tricks on editing yourself.

The last step for me now, always read it aloud because hearing it changes it. I'll discover all these things I couldn't have discovered because your eyes just skip over things naturally. This is how our eyes work. They fill in all these gaps. So I have to hear it and I'll be like, "oh, I'm repeating this word five times in a paragraph." I had no idea until I just kept saying it out loud.

No matter how many notes you get, something has to sing in you. And it sometimes will take me a couple weeks. I need time to let it melt. But if something makes me want to die, even after a few weeks, I'm not going to take that note. If you're like, "this note makes me want to die," please don't take it. It'll ruin your story. It'll be against who you are as a writer.

SSL: I was really struck by the empathy with which you drew Ingrid, who is very much this flawed character who is struggling with a lot of her problematic views on whiteness and whatnot. There is one section in particular where you delve into her past, where it addresses her growing up and developing her internalized racism, which I thought was really interesting. That's not really a topic that I feel like I've seen a lot written about. But it's also this very real thing that a lot of people of color, especially those who grew up in predominantly white spaces, have gone through and have had to grapple with. I was wondering if you could talk a little bit about the experience of writing that section.

EHC: In so many ways, I think I didn't want to write it, because I think it was sort of fulfilling audience expectations. If someone's an abuser or bully in a TV show, you bet on episode six, you get that flashback, and his father's beating him with a belt, and it's like, "ah, the world makes sense." Everything fits together. Everything has a clear cause and effect.

But I think our world is not actually like that. And I think I was resistant because I didn't want to fall into that trap of, "She's the way she is because of this very clear XYZ." And yet, I couldn't escape the fact that she was the way she was because of XYZ.

And so I think I cheated a little bit. I sort of put this line that was like, I think this is me. I think it's me talking. It's not necessarily the narrator anywhere. It's the line, "if a truth is repeated too often, it risks sounding untrue."

The problem of wanting to write something truthful, that a lot of other Asian kids have experienced, and then you're like—but I can't write that, my mom being mean to me, because that's been done before or something. I can't write about my parents forcing me to go to Kumon after school. That's such a cliche now. I don't know how to feel about this because I feel subjected to the same pressure. I also will feel this itch to try to write outside that. And yet, why? Why can't we write about real stuff? If a memoirist can write that, and have no qualms about it, because it's like, that's what happened to me, why in fiction do we necessarily have to avoid truth?

If your mom was mean to you, why do you feel you need to, for the sake of variety in Asian representation, make her like a white mom who served cookies after school, and was like, "tell me about your sex life" or something. I don't know. I feel like then we'll dig ourselves into this other hole,

So that's what I felt with Ingrid's backstory, and I in the end decided... I must be truthful to her character and this was the only way I could see how. So I just gave in. I gave in. In early drafts, I think that wasn't there. It seemed right in the end. It seemed I needed to, and I'm glad I wasn't on my high horse trying to avoid it.

SSL: I read that and thought, this really unlocks something about the character for me. So I needed to bring it up.

EHC: Think about how many novels might feature, let's say, a single white woman living in a city like New York, or L.A., who wears this type of clothing, goes to these types of restaurants—there's a million of those novels. Or like the white woman—they're all around white women—who's divorced and lonely. So she goes to Italy, or France, or Greece, to find this local man. So I feel like sometimes it is worth asking, are we unfairly put under a kind of magnifying glass where they seem to be able to write very similar tropes. Same thing, same thing, and how is that okay? I think we can butt up against these ideas and throw those stats at them. One day we should compile how many novels have been written about this type of lonely white woman in her 40s.

SSL: I feel all of this very strongly. I was in a workshop a few years ago, and I had submitted this story, there was another Asian American writer in the workshop, who said, "I feel like I've seen this story before, it sort of falls within the tropes that I've seen." And I was like, on the one hand, sometimes it is good to hear that feedback, because there are probably gaps in my literary knowledge at that point, but at the same time, you don't want to limit what you're writing about.

EHC: Exactly. You're writing about the thing that you are writing about because it's important to you in some way. And no one can write it the way you write it. His note should have been "how can we make this more specific?" If it's a mom, what about her is weird and unexpected? I find that very unhelpful, because no note should make you stop writing.

You should never give notes that make someone think, "I need to give up." And I've gotten a lot of notes that made me feel like that. But good notes should leave you itching to go to your WordDoc, should give you this idea. That's what a note should do, it should be generative. I'm sorry that he said something—literally, what is that comment gonna do?

It's like, useless. It's only one direction he's leading towards—I don't think this is worth writing. Which is so unfair. As readers, our duty is to ask, "how can we make this sing the way you want it to?"

SSL: Yeah. That's why it's so important to find your people and find your community who you do trust and can be vulnerable with.

EHC: Yes. Not all feedback is created equal. I also learned that, because I used to feel guilty. I was like, I'm not being a good writer if I don't weigh all of them equally and consider all of them.

And I'm like, no. If something makes me wanna die, I'm literally gonna throw it in the trash. And I think that is a good way to just go about it.

SL: Very good advice. You've been talking about this, but I love the kind of emphasis and importance that you place on the embodiment of a character. Especially because it's so apparent, it's so present in our daily lives, and yet can be so easily overlooked in our stories. It's something that I find myself having a lot of difficulty writing. I'm curious how you go about researching or writing about the bodies of characters that you might not be totally familiar with.

EHC: Oh, that's a great question. This is also something I feel I've been thinking about more recently. When I look back at certain stories now that I wrote when I was in the MFA program, I notice, this character doesn't have a body. I don't mention it at all.

With Ingrid's character—I think she was the first character that I tried really hard to do. I think at that point I couldn't even intellectualize it in terms of trying to embody her. It was more like, she's so nervous, and I don't know how to make that apparent, but besides the fact that her stomach is a wreck, her internal intestinal situation is a wreck, and it's not helped by all the junk food she eats. This is how I can show the audience she's not in a good place. She's very stressed out all the time.

So that was the first experiment. Later on I was like, "I wonder why haven't I done that with other characters?" In a story I wrote maybe like a year or so ago, I wrote from a perspective I'm really not used to writing.

It's an Asian man in his 60s. I was like, listen—at my age, I'm already feeling aches and pains. I think at 60, there's no way he's going to move through a day without feeling something. I didn't give him any kind of specific illness or injury or anything, but we're with him for this whole day, and he's standing a lot. So his legs really hurt and he just feels uncomfortable in that way and I try to build in those little moments. There's a great story by Nafissa Thompson-Spires in her collection *Heads of the Colored People*, where the main character has endometriosis, and I had never read anything that made me understand what it felt like. And it affects her life. So I think we don't have to put pressure on ourselves where every story should be super, super embodied?Maybe your character just has a headache at one point, and that's it.

SL: Sandra and I both went to your AWP panel where you moderated. It was such a thought provoking panel about reclaiming the Asian femme body in speculative fiction, and I guess just a general question about that is, how do you go about writing Asian femme bodies in speculative fiction?

EHC: I felt like all the authors on that panel, so talented and all right in such different ways—and it was great to hear how they approached it differently. I think for me—so these stories haven't been published—but one is about this Chinese, ba jiao gui, which is a banana tree ghost. It actually has roots in more southern China and Taiwan and Thailand, this creature.

She reads as, you might just imagine, the girl from The Ring. So she's got long hair. She's sort of terrifying. I put her in a sheet, and she's frightening looking, but she still reads as a small, short, pale-skinned East Asian woman. That's how she reads and so in that sense, people might slot her into those stereotypes of women who look like that?

And so I had so much fun making her character gross. She just pops out her eyeballs all the time and, and inside her mouth—whenever she opens her mouth—she has this suctioning void. It's basically like a black hole. So she can't feel food, but she loves eating.

She's able to levitate too, I gave her that. So I was just having a lot of fun with making her body not a sexual site. And I got to make her weird and cool and I got to think of that type of body in a way I never had.

So here's the thing. She's a mythological ghost who's adopted by white parents, and they bring her back to Indiana, and they enroll her in a suburban high school.

So let's say I took out the speculative part of that, and she was just a teenage Chinese girl that was adopted, same exact scenario. To stay within the bounds of reality, guys and girls would have said messed up things to her, and it would have been a very different type of story.

In the beginning, there's this one cool girl who's actually Chinese-American and adopted, but she's not a creature. She's the cool girl, and she's really mean to her. So at first you think Banana (her nickname) is just gonna be bullied.

But I had so much fun with it, because she can do all this cool stuff and she terrifies people. They're afraid of her, she actually ascends, she just keeps getting cooler and has a sort of respect, and I think none of this could have been possible with a realist story. But because I opened up that door, I had options. She actually identifies as ace, asexual. People ask her to prom because she's so cool, and people like, fight over her to go to prom, and she's like, "no, I'm ace"—and I love that part. I love that, and it just made so much sense. I remember that was a couple drafts in where I was like, "oh yeah, she's asexual because she's her body". Like sex is not a thing for her, it doesn't even compute. And so I think it was thrilling to write for the first time a completely desexualized, Asian femme body.

Maybe we write these stories—a lot of us and on that panel—because it's something we can't have in real life. It's like this wish fulfillment like wow, what would it be like?

SL: You've mentioned multiple times how you started from scratch for each draft of *Disorientation* and never copied anything over from the previous draft. First of all, it's an impressive feat. But I'm curious to know if you have ever gone back to those drafts and taken anything from them, like specific lines, or images, or metaphors, and used them in other creative works.

EHC: Yes. I did do that. I didn't allow myself when I was drafting, wouldn't look at it. Can't open it. It's dead to me. Draft, draft, draft. And then when that new draft was done, I'd reread the old one and see, is there anything that actually fits that I kind of forgot or could be salvaged?

Between the first and second version—maybe not a lot. A lot of it changed, and the tense changed. For specific lines, I think it was hard to copy over. The tone had changed a lot.

And then from the second to the third version, there was a part I kept. Ingrid was maybe thinking this in the second version, which isn't in the first person. And so, since it really wasn't about her, I could just copy it over.

One is when she's witnessing Timothy talk to these Barnes students about affirmative action. And he's just like, gunning for affirmative action. That speech that he gives—that didn't change.

SL: There's this thing when you kill off your darlings for one story, I put them in a different document. I like this image, or the flow of this sentence that might not work for this draft, but someday I'm probably going to use it. Do you ever find yourself doing that with those previous drafts?

EHC: I always think I will. If I'm editing a short story, I'll have a deletions doc open, so I'll just cut something and immediately throw it in that, the graveyard. And I think I do it for peace of mind, but I never read through them.

I don't know if this is true or not, but I had this feeling of well, since I keep writing, probably the stuff I'm coming up with now is better than the stuff I thought of that year or the year before. Which I don't think is true at all, actually, but I think I just tell myself that to save myself the work of going through it and reading it and trying to find how it could fit in again.

I want to fly through, in the sense of, I'm gonna let fate decide. If I'm writing something new and this sentence emerges from the recesses of my brain and my memories. Oh yeah, I remember that, okay, it was meant to be.

And so I just let myself off easy because I have so much deleted stuff. I love to delete. We haven't talked in so long, but this incredible, incredible writer who I met at NYU, we were in our very first workshop together, he, right off the bat, everything he submitted was stunning. I mean—I was so in awe of him.

I remember he just kept submitting new versions of the beginning of this chapter. And by the third time, I thought, every one is perfect, every one is so good. Why, why do you keep doing it instead of the next one? And he said this thing—I wish I could go back and record it perfectly, so I'm going to butcher it—"every unexplored possibility is too seductive to ignore."

And I was floored. I had been writing from this point of view. I had been writing from a space of, I need to know what's right, right off the bat, and I need to stick to that plan. And I need to know where I'm going and that's it. But he wrote from a point of view that's almost more like TV writing, that you entertain every idea.

That's why you need 12 people in a room, that's why it's very hard to do it on your own, because you need people to just like, throw it, pitch, pitch, pitch, the most wildest thing, and then in the end, eliminate, until you get to the thing that can resist elimination. And I realized he was doing that on his own, with a novel. Whereas I wanted to make it easy for myself, I wanted to think a little, brainstorm and be like, I figured it out. This is how it should be written. And this is the path I'm taking. Less work for me. And here he was so dedicated to the story that he refused to not explore everything it could be. Very few writers can do that. It's hard. But I never forgot that and I've held on to that this whole time. Once in a while I'll be like, "if I was him, what would I do?" I'm gonna open that door. That door's kind of scary. I've got deadlines. I'm tired, but sometimes he's right. That seduction, I just let it open a little bit.

SSL: Our final couple of questions are about your upcoming work. You mentioned last night that it's a multi-genre story collection, which is super exciting. I'm curious what some of the different forms your stories take are and if you could talk a little bit about that.

EHC: Ooh, yes, yes. This collection—I started calling it that because I feel like it's gonna be a mixed bag of nuts. I have what I hope will be that expose of the Asian KKK member, there's the banana tree ghost story, there's a fairy tale that begins more like a Chinese folk tale because I was really interested in these two really old forms that date back hundreds of years—how they were written and how I can make the worlds collide. So I had a lot of fun with it.

So it's a big mixed bag, but I actually wrote quite a few of the stories when I was an MFA student, and then have thrown out quite a few of them and wrote new ones. So I think this collection—I don't know what, how to describe it.

It's just interesting to present a work that feels like it's pulled from so many different parts of yourself and your life. When it comes out, it will be presented in a way that this is the EHC now who wrote it, but a lot of these stories I was at a different place when I wrote it, and some of the stories I've had to revamp completely. But other ones I'm going to stay true to that EHC at that time, and respect how she felt about this story and why she wrote it. I think it will be—hopefully—a healthy way for me to not pick it apart.

Because with the ones I'm revamping, I sense this dangerous line where I can't even tell if in two different paragraphs, have I changed the tone? Because I'm writing so my head is in a different place. I'm like, will someone read it and be like, this doesn't make sense.

And so I think I'm recognizing that and trying to be be very careful not to over-edit, like a carcass—you don't want to edit your stuff until it's a carcass, and it's unrecognizable to you.

SSL: It's so interesting to look at your writing from different periods of your life. I feel like the writer you might have been even a year ago is just so different.

EHC: I agree. I agree because we change all the time. We change our minds, our moods, and our tastes too. Think about the music you were into as a teen, in every year of your teens was probably changing so much.

Something we should talk about more is how books are seen as so permanent, like a calling card, like a permanent this is you. It's me or where my head was mostly at a very specific time. So I think books should be seen more like photos. It releases the pressure. With friends, we've talked about when the deadline is coming up you really can no longer edit this. You're in the final pass. It needs to go to the printers. At that stage there's this anxiety of, "but what if I still want to change something?" And the fact that you even found one thing to change at this stage—it worries you. I think we've got to take the pressure off ourselves and be like, you can't expect this book to stand for you for the rest of your life.

Because that means you wouldn't change as a person. So let the book become a snapshot of who you were when you were writing it.

Near Enough

Maz Do

Eka felt the pressure on Tuesday morning as if she'd swallowed something large and heavy. The stomach pangs were so severe she wondered if it was appendicitis. But didn't appendicitis begin on the right side of the body? Had she eaten too much dairy? Hadn't she eaten enough? She tried to ignore it – sort files, mark spreadsheets – but the pain was relentless. Eka unbuttoned her wool skirt, yanked down her black tights and scarfed a dry sleeve of saltines. Nothing alleviated her suffering.

Eka counted each second 'till six o'clock. Stared mournfully at the lithe women swanning past her desk. She was sure one of these women carried painkillers in their purse. But she couldn't bring herself to ask. Here, her only goal was to make herself innocuous. In America the only words said were those which meant nothing at all. Her life was circumscribed by fear. She was afraid of her coworkers, especially the women—formidable, tall, leering creatures who would not hesitate to cut her from nose to navel if she simply looked at them the wrong way.

She didn't yet know what kind of American woman she would become. She had moved to California five years ago to attend UC Irvine. Then she'd graduated and taken the first job offered to her. At first, she celebrated. She had not squandered her parents' money, as was their expectation. She had acquired a visa, a means of financial security, and a dream. And it was always this dream, however nebulous, which she tried to articulate in her letters back to her family.

Eka wrote furiously, tearing reams of paper from the yellow legal pads she smuggled out of the firm's supply closets. It took three stamps to send a letter to her brother in London and five to send one all the way back to Jambi. Weeks, months passed before her letters arrived. Often, her mother relayed, how they arrived with yellow stains splashed across the front as if the postman thought piss of her dreams.

Eka waited patiently her apartment's mailroom for letters to return. When they arrived, she carried them around all day like talismans, wearing down the corners with her fingers until she felt she couldn't take it any longer and ripped them open.

How much are you making these days? When are you coming back home? Will you get married? Do you think you'll have a baby? Will you stay in California forever? Don't you miss your family? Do you pray to God every night?

Endless questions, endless. All in the careful, manicured cursive Eka's mother learned in grade school from the nuns. Her mother had only grown more obstinate in an empty home, her children distant, orbiting satellites, thousands of kilometers away. Eka wondered if her mother was lonely; she couldn't imagine her father without a paper obscuring his face. Sometimes Eka phoned, but only a handful of times, since both mother and daughter agreed paying three dollars per minute just to whisper static to one another, was highway robbery.

Secretly, Eka craved her father's voice. All her life he had been an opaque figure, a distant deity. Only now as an adult did she feel curiosity about the man who'd raised her. She would have paid any exorbitant fee to hear the quiet rasp of his voice.

But Eka didn't dare ask, so her mother never put him on. Instead, the two of them wrote through the days, which stretched into weeks and months and eventually years.

While at work, Eka kept the pain, held it inside her and smiled through dinner.

That night, as if to reward her restraint, the pain subsided and ushered her into a dreamless sleep. As soon as she woke, she zipped herself into her skirt and drove over to the office to greet clients and file papers.

It was during Eka's lunch break that she opened a letter which contained no questions at all. The handwriting on the page was neat but fragile – as if the hand that had written it shook with a faint tremor.

Pa caught a cold last month. They've kept him at the hospital just to be safe.

The doctors say he'll be home by the end of the week.

I've been drinking Milo instead of coffee. You can't buy Milo, can you? Do they stock it in the stores? Do you still remember the taste?

LONGING

Happy birthday Eka. Thank God for all your blessings.

Out of the envelope fell a blue slip of paper, tented in half, for one thousand dollars.

One thousand dollars.

She wondered if it was an error. A misplaced zero – perhaps two. She wracked her brain to remember the last time she received a birthday note from her parents, let alone money. This much money. The date on the envelope was stamped April 12th. Her birthday was in February. She felt it again: a slow pulse, her familiar friend. The pain twisted, wrenched her insides. She bit the palm of her hand to keep herself from crying out.

When she regained the ability to speak, she told the Claremont graduate to watch the desk and marched out the double doors. She sprinted to the nearest phone booth.

She racked her brain over who to call first. A doctor? Her mother? She didn't know which she feared more; the fee or her mother's admonitions over wasted time and money. Her fingers hovered over the rotary dial.

The operator, three rings, then a brash, familiar voice.

"Halo. Eka?! Say that again? You sound out of breath. Don't tell me you've gained weight." Her brother's laugh rang, taut and tinny from a thousand kilometers away. His voice sounded muffled, like he had food in his mouth.

"Vincent," she gasped. All the while the pain stabbed her gut. "Listen to me. Mama's sent me a letter—" She paused and wondered if mentioning the money was a good idea. He had never hesitated to take from her.

"Eka, don't be daft. You and Mama, with all your letters. It's a small cold. I've talked to him. Talked to the doctors too. He's already home from the hospital – didn't you know?"

She paused. She didn't answer.

She heard him swallow. "Exactly, dik. You worry over nothing."

"But I didn't—"

"My God, you women would go on forever if we let you." He laughed at his bad joke. "Give Mama a call, okay? Make sure you brush up on your Bible-reading first. Meet her where she's at."

Then she heard the dial tone.

It was already too late to call Jambi. Eka ran back to the office to grab her things. She mumbled to her supervisor something about bleeding to which he shuddered and waved her away—"Take the rest of the day off," he said.

With little else to do, Eka drove to Aldrich Park. She and her university friends spent long, meandering afternoons there. Though most of them were gone now – back to their homes, to new jobs or other schools —

at least the park remained familiar.

She stomped around the pond, deliberately scuffing up the thick, glossy heels of her Mary Janes, ones she'd bought at Payless. At the time they'd seemed to strike the right tone of sobriety and class, but they subsequently revealed themselves to be simultaneously old-fashioned, childish and $7.99 for that reason.

Her mother, her brother: all their lives they'd shut her out. This, they did routinely, for them it was as natural as brushing one's teeth. Now they had neglected to tell her about her father's grievous illness, so serious he'd had to stay in the hospital. She was angry, feverishly so and the anger mingled with her pain to produce a new, acute feeling. Were they trying to punish her? What for? How and when had she sinned – by moving too far from home, by choosing the wrong profession, by refusing to marry her brother's ugly friend, that businessman from Jakarta with his big teeth and black pores and inability to look her in the eyes? Or had the sin occurred earlier, was she doomed from the start? Did it begin and end with the absence of that ghostly appendage, swinging between her legs?

Eka felt like taking her shoes off and dropping them into the scum-covered water.

But she knew she was incapable. Too rash, too American. So she paced instead. Eka screamed, then, from her stomach, long and loud. The noise startled the flock, which set off into the sky. She watched them rise higher and higher as the scream faded and went cold in her throat.

It was sunset, now, and the light glanced off of the rippling water, silhouetting the ducks. Dusk here, dawn there.

Behind her rang the chime of a bicycle bell; behind that echoed the soft thumps of a basketball, rubber squeaking, feet negotiating pavement. She breathed deeply, inhaling the smell of grass, earthy and cool.

Her chin trembled, so she pinched her cheeks pink.

Thank you, God, for all my blessings.

The pain stayed with her that night and persisted through Thursday. To pass the time she imagined the pain as different objects: a hot iron ball, a spiked mallet, a handful of Chinese throwing stars one saw in kung-fu films. During her lunch break she hobbled over to the drugstore, but all they had on hand were chalky, pastel discs and an unctuous pink milk whose very sight made her feel vomitous. She thought of jamu her mother brewed whenever one of them fell ill. She could taste the yellow, the tingling spice, the opposite of the sterile fluorescence of the drugstore. Eka staggered out of the Walgreens empty-handed, clutching her stomach to keep from falling over. The minute she returned to the office her supervisor dropped a stack of invoices in front of her so high it obstructed her view of her besieged coworker.

As the hours passed the pain slid down her body. By six, it rested inside her pelvis. She lay awake, tossing and sweating and wondered if its descent might herald its end. She did not permit herself to become too hopeful. If there was anything she learned since she'd moved to America, it was never to become too hopeful.

On Friday, Eka woke to find the pain in stasis. It neither intensified nor abated. Instead it remained firmly stuck below her stomach, right above her bladder. The pain made her think of her father, lying in his miasma. She tried to remember his face, but the image of him kept slipping from her, like the memory of a dream which disintegrates upon waking. Then she felt ashamed of her own suffering, of her body's narcissism. Yes, bear it, she whispered to herself. Bear it through. She resolved to swallow the pain.

At twelve o'clock, Eka passed out next to the water cooler. For the firm, the event was the drama of the afternoon; it derailed lunch by fifteen minutes and forced HR to reconsider its foreign outreach program as well as its policy on maternity leave.

Despite his better judgment, Eka's supervisor sent her home. "Come in early Monday," he called after her on her way out the door. Perhaps she was hallucinating but she swore she saw, in his wave goodbye, her blue work visa stuck between his fingers.

Back at the apartment, Eka drew a tepid bath and lay in the tub until her fingers went pruny. Then she climbed out, made herself a cup of Lipton and lay down with a cold compress on her forehead and a hot one on her belly.

Her febrile thoughts flit from her mother to her father to her brother. For years she had suppressed them in order to bear the endless passage of time, at the end of which lay that shifting, uncertain dream. She had kept her head down and worked. She made them ghosts in her mind. Now, their faces danced upon the ceiling, mouths moving wordlessly. No matter how hard she tried, she couldn't make out what they were saying. An hour passed this way, perhaps two. When she couldn't bear it, Eka turned her head and buried her face into the pillow.

Eka sat up, alert, blinded by light. For a moment she thought she had been deposited into a nightmare before the car's headlights beamed past the window, leaving the room in darkness. She tenderly touched her swollen stomach and winced at the pain, which throbbed so hard in her pelvis she swore it must have burst a blood vessel.

Perhaps the pain lanced her from within, so blood coated her liver, her kidneys. Internal bleeding was strange to think about, for it hinted at the fact that one's body was a mystery to oneself, that the body was capable of betrayal. She felt herself a doomed Trojan horse.
She thought of her own father, swaddled in blue sheets. It was then that she understood he would leave them later that evening. She was certain, too, that she wasn't the only woman who knew.

One ring.

"You're up late, Eka," her mother said, sounding very much awake. She spoke in English, stiff and formal. Her mother sometimes did this, and only since Eka had moved to America. It was a habit Eka hated, it bewildered her, she took it as though her mother were saying: look, see how far we are? Here's the distance.

"I can't sleep," Eka responded, refusing the English.

"Sleep is good for your skin. You should deposit that check." Her mother switched, too and so did her tone; she was gently scolding.

"Mama. How is he?"

"Pa is sleeping. I wanted him home. I insisted. That hospital – they don't know. I've been with him for forty years. I know."

"Can I talk to him?"

Her voice grew thin and faint. "Don't worry about Pa," her mother said. Eka bit her lip. "I can book a flight. I'll fly out tonight."

"With what money?"

Eka didn't answer.

Her mother's voice grew stern. "Don't be stupid. That check is for you and your future. Pray to God, that's all we can do now."

"Is Vincent there?"

There was a long pause on the other end of the line. Her mother's fingers, she thought, crocheting tulips. No, she revised: working her rosary beads.

"He flew in last night," she said at last.

The pain gripped Eka's stomach. "Last night. You could have told me."

Her mother's voice hardened to impatience. "You could have called."

Her mother was right. She could have. She had contemplated calling home for the past four days, had picked up the phone a dozen times but always stopped short of dialing. Every time she picked up the phone, her head began to spin.

I've been busy. I've been ill. I've been scared. Paltry excuses.

"Let me talk to him," she pleaded. "I should have called, but please."

"He'll hardly be able to say a thing."

"Why didn't you tell me?" Eka felt like a child again; small, inconsolable, ridiculous.

"Everything happened so fast. You're so far away."

"I'm not," she said, and her throat pinched holding back a sob. "I'm near enough."

Her mother had always been brutal. Why should death receive special treatment?

She heard her mother call his name softly, in a faraway voice. It was the placating tone she'd always used with him, so unlike the way she commanded her children.

"Your daughter wants to speak with you," she said. Eka heard the rustling of sheets and a crackling sound as a mouth was brought to the receiver.

"Pa?"

His breathing was heavy, familiar. The same steady breath which perpetually smelled of whiskey and tobacco now whispered in her ear strange portents. "Eka? Why aren't you sleeping? Are you cold?"

No matter how many times she told them how warm it was in California they'd refused to believe her. Every Christmas her mother asked if it snowed.

"It's ten degrees, Pa. Are you comfortable? What are you doing?"

"I'm lying here. Mama won't let me get up." He moaned in his usual way.

They talked about nothing at all. Eka sat and listened while watching a group of ants make their arduous way up the stucco. Even though for him it was the middle of the afternoon she wanted to believe it was morning.

She wanted to believe that the sun would have just breached the horizon, just begun to stretch its flat rays across the pasar, the alleys full of stray dogs, through her mother's garden. She thought of her parents' window which always caught the first, best light and of her father who liked to sleep on the left side of the bed so as to see the rising sun in all its yellow glory, amber like enriched yolks. The light, warming his hand, his arm. Not his face, though. Not just yet.

She let him murmur in her ear. At last the pain in her stomach dulled, ebbed from her body. She sank to the kitchen floor and listened to the sound of his papery voice, soft and slow. Outside the rain picked up again. It drummed soft fingers against the roof. Among the shifting clouds bloomed the pockmarked moon. She imagined it was the sun. She imagined herself right there, beside him.

Eka sat on the cold tile and prayed, thanked him for all she had.

After Hours Elsewhere

Alexandra Watson

I aim for bed, the bar is on the way
And you. I know that bright red dress. Fox trap
collarbones I slice myself open on–
I always remember blood. I walk past
first, then turn and compliment your work. I
look you in the jaw and say hello. I
think I said too much. The animal in
my eyelid flees. My mouth too hot.

In the dream, you keep me from crossing the
stream. We speak without words like mushrooms,
like trees. You spin me around the hollow
of a brick courtyard & the cold earth thaws
A thumb swipes stray mascara. The filters
break off. You leave a new stain on my teeth.

The Fifth-Grade Lesbian

Lupita Aquino

I was christened a lesbian when I was ten years old. My two best friends in fifth grade were the priestess who overlooked my early baptism; they immersed me in a circular pool with jeers and laughter.

The memory returns to me when my wife and I realize our son might attend my old elementary school. But the memory returns not at the mention of my old school, but when my wife leans in to kiss me.

When I close my eyes to receive the touch of her lips I identify a twinge of shame that didn't feel present between us before the rediscovery of this memory. Shame drops into my stomach like a heavy rock. I hear the laughter echoing, I feel the rippled dents of the beige-colored concrete walls. I want to melt into those walls and disappear. The knot in my throat tightens but I do not let the tears flow.

My lesbian baptism happened on a Monday. I hid back tears behind my misshapen bangs. I tried joining in on the laughter too, as if I was in on a big staged joke. I pretended it was someone else we were laughing at and taunting. I was good at being quiet, at blending in. Good at going with what the other kids said and did. Good at making myself the joke. Good at hiding. Staying quiet and hidden was essential to surviving school, especially if you were a brown, chubby, anxious and awkward

little girl. That combination was unforgiving.

It was the backing away as if I had shit my pants, the finger-pointing, and the hollering from a circle of kids with me in the middle, that clued me into the fact that there was something wrong about being called a lesbian. I stood in that circle of taunts laughing at myself hoping to hide in plain sight because I had no idea what I was being called or why. I was hoping this term somehow meant something that was easy to fix, like being called stinky. If I was the stinky kid, I could just go home, lock myself in the bathroom for over an hour and finally run to my Mami's room to steal her perfume. I could spray her Estée Lauder Beautiful, that she only ever sprayed for very special occasions, all over and never be called stinky again. Being enfolded in the flumes on a perfume only used by older white women could have become my resolution.

But it was the months that followed after being called a lesbian in the fifth grade, that made me understand it wasn't something I could fix. All the Estée Lauder Beautiful in the world wouldn't save me from being the fifth grade lesbian. I became permanently and indefinitely marked for the rest of the year. No one talked to me anymore. No one played with me and if a ball would happen to roll anywhere near me, that ball immediately ceased to exist too. Being called a lesbian became something that destroyed my early friendships with other girls too. It planted a tiny seed of shame I'd buried deep inside my esophagus that would slowly start to grow as I came into myself and learned that this thing I was called so early on was true all along. What I had missed is that seed became a sleeping volcano.

That was 30-something years ago and I have never returned to this memory. Now, it haunts me. It sits with me begging my mind to replay that singular memory over and over like some cringe holiday movie on a network channel no one is watching. With each play, the opening credits appear in bold white over a black background: "I know why you didn't sleepover. It's because you're a lesbian….."

How was I discovered so early?

How was it that *they* knew before I even knew?

Was it something I said or did?

Did I do something wrong?

This is what haunts me. The shame, I can feel it boiling.

My best friend Wendy was celebrating her 11th birthday with a sleepover. We had talked about it for weeks. The plan: we'd stay up late watching TV until we knew her parents were asleep. We'd have a pillow fight. We'd make prank calls to random numbers listed in the thick phonebook with thin pages. We'd prank our own houses too. I imagined how the entire evening would play out. I didn't know this then but when I'm in my early 30s I'll learn about how some people actively try to imagine different scenarios in order to find relief from an obsessive fear. This makes sense as to why the evening ended the way it did for me.

But here's what I imagined the sleepover to be like then: one of us would dial and say into the receiver, "Is your refrigerator running?" We would quietly wait for a "yes" and bust out "well you better go out and catch it!"

We'd laugh well into the night and just like in the movies, it would end with us whispering our secrets and vowing to be best friends forever. That vow excited me most; I was desperate for friends and eager for another girl to call me her best friend.

I especially wanted that with Sonya.

Sonya was Wendy's second-in-command. But there was nothing "second" about her. She was special. Sonya knew the corniest yo mama jokes and would obliterate our mothers. Her laugh was infectious. A laugh that started as a small snicker and grew into a roaring belly laugh with snorts making it so that even when her jokes weren't funny, her laughter was enough to get us all cackling like a pack of hyenas. Next to me, Sonya was slightly shorter with a perfect black bob-shaped hairstyle that fell around her cheeks and just above her shoulders. Sonya's laughter might have been infectious but it was her smile that was captivating. She had two front teeth that were slightly bigger than the rest but when she smiled her full lips that naturally puckered hid them so her smile resembled any model in a Colgate commercial. She was perfect.

Sonya disarmed the boys. She demanded space and challenged them. She didn't know how to play basketball but she'd still step into their games by stealing their ball and bulldozing her way into them to take a shot. A shot she would end up missing every single time. Her energy brought the boys in and we'd giggled anytime one of them tried to come over and talk to her afterwards. She wasn't interested in talking to them, she only wanted to mess with them. She used to tell us her older sister would say to never let a boy think you like him, instead show him you don't care.

But the thing that made Sonya so special to me wasn't necessarily that energy. It was the fact that when it was just us, she'd hold my hand as we walked down the hallways. Sonya loved hugs and she'd wrap herself around me in a tight embrace after every hello and goodbye. Between Sonya and I physical space didn't exist. Before Sonya, I had never experienced that level of physical affection with another girl. We were tight. We were close. So close, we shared jawbreakers the size of baseballs. We'd take turns licking the colorful orbs; we'd watch each other lick the jawbreaker until it got small enough to fit in our mouths. We were convinced we'd find something special in the core.

So I was convinced that Wendy's sleepover would seal our friendship forever.

There was one small problem--I had never slept over at anyone else's home before. It wasn't that there weren't opportunities to attend sleepovers that kept me a sleepover virgin. And it was easy to place the blame on my strict Mexican parents. Often, I'd lie to my primas when they'd beg me to ask for permission. It was an easy lie to tell: though Mami caved to my adorable prima's pleas sometimes, but Papi would remain tight-lipped. His silence meant it was a "no" and my Mami never fought it. That's how I remained a sleepover virgin for years.

I was the problem. I couldn't handle the idea of staying in a stranger's house. That was the epidermis layer of it. The dermis layers, hidden deeply underneath, held my secret fear of the darkness; specifically the darkness that penetrated a home. I didn't exactly fear the idea of the dark, I feared what could *happen* in that darkness. My experiences so far in the darkness had taught me that it twisted people into *something* else. In the darkness, a doorknob of a locked room would feverishly jiggle for minutes that felt like hours before stopping completely. In the darkness, a little girl would be bolted out of sleep in a deep panic by the wrestling of the doorknob. In the darkness, a little girl would try to recite prayers to a God she learned wasn't listening. I couldn't let anyone else see that I was that little girl. I wasn't willing to share the secret of why the darkness had groomed me into these robotic reactions.

Not Wendy but especially not Sonya.

But I feared being friendless and alone more than I feared the darkness and my secrets. So I gathered the courage and said to my parent's "It's one night. Everyone in school does it all the time." When that didn't work, I reminded them of every single time my primas would ask if I could sleep over their house and they wouldn't let me. I parroted Mami's older brother's pleas on behalf of his daughters back to them "déjalas que sean niñas". I demanded that they let me be a girl just this one time and then to finish my argument completely I hit them with a gut punch I had learned never to use - "you guys just don't understand that this isn't Mexico". And that did it. Their mini translator and navigator between languages and cultures calling them out like that was enough to finally make them say "esta bien."

There was a lot riding on this sleepover. Before Wendy and Sonya, there was Yasmin. Yasmin taught me the power a girl could hold over another girl. Fear. Fear became the power with which she kept me close. I met Yasmin in my Tia C's child care business. She ran it out of my godmother's house. It was packed with family, neighborhood kids, and children of other immigrant families our parents befriended. Tia C would watch more than ten of us. Different kids always coming in and out, it was all very Lord-of-the-fly-ish.

I was in the second grade when Yasmin appeared at my Tia C's door with her loud Mami. Yasmin was much older and having recently migrated from Mexico, she was held a few grades back since she struggled with English.

Yasmin overpowered everyone at Tia C's but she took a special interest in me. We fell into a pattern. Anything Yasmin said to do, I would do. I became Yasmin's hands. When she said we needed to beat up another girl, I hit that girl over and over again even when she curled her body into herself on the floor. I didn't stop until Tia C stopped us. The girl had done nothing to me. But Yasmin said to hit her, so I hit her.

One day, Yasmin called me into the bathroom at Tia C's. She locked the door behind me and pointed to the toilet water. It was bright pink with thick clots of burgundy and black sprinkled on the top. Her period. "Si no lo miras, te lo unto. ¡Míralo!", she said. I stared at the toilet bowl for as long as she needed me to, so she wouldn't smear the blood all over me. Yasmin laughed when she saw the fear in my eyes. It wasn't until I started crying that she'd finally opened the door and run out.

This became her abusive and sorted version of a friendship pact with me. A ritual she'd perform to keep me in line. It was the only type of friendship I knew. A friendship driven and held together by fear. A friendship in which I'm a pawn to a queen. But even that friendship ended.

One day we bumped into each other in the bathroom. Not at Tia C's, but at school. The sight of her in the school's bathroom filled me with so much terror. The anticipation of seeing her blood pool burgundy and black made me wet my pants. I stood in front of her, my pants soaked with urine, dripping slowly onto the bathroom floor.

She yelled "¡cochina! Te measte" and ran out of the school bathroom so that no one would see her with a girl who wet her pants. Not even all the previous months of being secretly subjected to her period, made out to be her pawn ready to protect the queen, was enough to be seen with someone like me. So the sleepover became my chance at redemption. The chance not only at real friendship but the chance to prove there wasn't anything wrong with me.

For the sleepover, my parents bought me a brand new lavender sleeping bag with small printed white flowers. Why did I need a sleeping bag if I could take with me the huge cobijas with an eagle on it? My parents asked. "We're sleeping on the floor", I said. They didn't get it. We left Mexico so I could sleep on a real plush mattress, not on the ground and this became my reminder to them of why it was important I have this quintessential "American" experience.

As the sleepover day approached, Mami still wasn't convinced. Her doubts should have been a sign for me."Estas segura", "Vas estar en casa ajena" and "Que pasa si te da miedo?", she'd ask the week before the sleepover. But I had facts prepared to fire back:

1. La Wendy's house was five minutes away. If needed, I could walk home.

2. La Wendy's mom was nice. She always popped out with a big smile and waved at the school bus driver.

Then there was the last and most important reason:

3. "Va ir La Sonya, Mami" I'd say to her with pleading eyes.
Mami had met Wendy and Sonya a couple of times when they'd come over after school. She'd understood we became close like a pod of dolphins. But Mami never had much to say about them. She would disappear whenever they'd come over. She didn't ask questions about them or about any other friendships I had in school.

It was my Mami who dropped me off at Wendy's. I had to talk her into coming to the door instead of leaving me to walk up on my own. Mami avoided talking to other parents, afraid to fumble the few words she knew in English. I got used to sensing her embarrassment, always ready to step in and pick up the conversation. At drop-off, my Mami said a quick "hello" and "thank you" before giving me the typical pórtate-bien-estás-en casa-ajena look.

Wendy and Sonya rushed to greet me at the door with Wendy's cousins and sisters in tow. I wave goodbye to my Mami and get rushed into running upstairs to Wendy's room while Wendy's mother yells behind us "Girls we are going to be making our pizzas soon so be back down here in five minutes".

I'm back there, a fifth-grader, in Wendy's bedroom.

I am frozen with reality sinking in. Her room is nothing like my room. There is no nightlight. The wood-paneled walls make the room darker. The room will turn pitch dark when the lights turn off.

Everyone sets up their sleeping bags. Sonya rushes to take my hand. "Sleep next to me," she says as she guides me to a spot by the door next to her sleeping bag. I feel a rush of warmth. I sense Wendy watching us from her bed. "Girls, come down for pizza," Wendy's mom yells.

We make pizzas and sing Happy Birthday. It's almost time for the sleepover part. My heart thumps a little harder.

Wendy's mom saying, "Alright girls lights will go off in ten minutes. Get dressed and ready for bed." causes my heart to thump harder. In the bathroom, my mind won't quiet down as I slide into my PJs: What about the pillow fight? Watching TV late into the night? I had rehearsed the entire night in my mind for days, there was supposed to be more time, more activities to make it so we didn't all lay in the darkness together so quickly. It wasn't supposed to go this way. The darkness wasn't supposed to be coming so quickly. My eyes meet Sonya's as I step out of the bathroom. She smiles. My heart settles.

As long as Sonya is sleeping next to me, I can do this.

"Why aren't you sleeping next to me, Sonya?" Wendy asks as she approaches once we have settled into our bags. "It's *my* birthday. *She* pees on herself." Wendy points her finger at me.

"You don't want to sleep next to her," Wendy and Sonya both laugh. I try to laugh too but my face goes hot.

I lower my eyes and mumble "That's not true." Even if it was true. But how could she have known? She didn't know Yasmin.

Sonya looks at me and then at Wendy and says "I wasn't going to sleep next to her. She tried to get me to. Did you see her grab my hand? There's something weird about her." I can feel a knot form in my throat. It's the knot that usually shows up when I am about to cry.

But Sonya was the one that grabbed my hand. Sonya's the one that reaches to hug me at school. Why is it weird now?? Was it wrong of me to imagine that perhaps during the sleep over, her warm body next to me, might help fight off any fears the darkness might pop out? Was it wrong or weird of me to hope that maybe during the night she might reach for me like she does at school before we both fell asleep?.Was it wrong to hope or imagine she would do that sometime during the night after we whispered our secrets to each other? I wanted this all to end up with us being best friends forever which I thought might be sealed by her sharing something with me she's never told anyone before. None of the night was supposed to go like this. When the lights go off, I curl next to the door. Alone. Sonya moves her sleeping bag next to Wendy's bed. I can hear them whispering. I try hard not to cry but the tears come in hot.

The darkness is here. The whispering is just loud enough for me to make out what is being said. Wendy and Sonya are talking about me. Sonya is telling Wendy about the times she's hugged me and how weird I made it. Sonya's telling her that when she hugs me, I hug her back too tightly. That I make her hold hands with me and she thinks I might be "obsessed with her or something". They both agree I'm weird and that it was a mistake to invite me. The other girls start to chime in but I've tuned them all out because I can feel the darkness starting to claim its rights to my body again because of the whispering.

My heart is thumping faster and faster in my chest, hard like a jackhammer. The panic that the darkness brings, has found its way in the room with us. The darkness has done it again, turned people that I thought I was safe with into something else. The darkness has willed them against me. With this panic comes a flood of thoughts, what if I pee myself in my sleep? Sonya thinks I'm weird. Why am I weird? There's something wrong with me. I'm not normal. I ruined this. I ruin everything. The harder I try not to cry, the harder the tears come.

I grab my sleeping bag and push myself out of the dark room and into the lit hallway straight down the stairs.

When Wendy's Mom sees me, she throws questions at me like bullets "Are you okay? Did the girls hurt you? What's wrong?"

In the light, I settle down enough and say, " I want to go home."

Mami picks up the phone on the second ring. My crying picks up again as Wendy, Sonya, and the girls all watch me from the stairs. My Mami shows up 15 minutes later. Still crying, I pick up my sleeping bag and head out the door. Mami hangs back and mumbles quiet sorries to Wendy's Mom and the girls.

In the car ride home, Mami doesn't say a thing. She doesn't scold me or ask me what happened. She doesn't even give me her typical "ya ves" which she reserves for moments like this because she turned out to be right. In the years to come, that evening along with a handful of other failed sleepover attempts, will turn into a running joke between us. "Mi niña nunca pudo dormir en casa ajena porque extrañaba mucho a su Mami", she'll say. And I will laugh and lean in to hug her to reassure her the reason I failed those sleepovers was simply because I missed her too much and not because of anything else.

But that night after returning to my own bed, I let the darkness continue its claim to my body. The panic backed out of my chest and settled into a whirlpool of thoughts in my mind. I stayed up all night hugging my teddy bear and thinking about Sonya. Replaying every hug she's ever given me. Every instance when she's been nice to me. Hoping that when Monday comes, no one will have remembered the sleepover.

"Stop. Don't come any closer to me. I know why you didn't sleepover. It's because you're a lesbian." It was Sonya who christened me first, that following Monday in the hallway while we waited for the cafeteria to open.

"That's why you left the sleepover. You like me."

It's the first thing Sonya says to me as I approach her and Wendy outside of the classroom. I found them leaning into each other whispering about something. I was hoping they were whispering something about the teacher or another kid, like we normally do while waiting for lunch to start. I thought we could pretend the sleepover never happened.

But Sonya and Wendy stand in front of me, suddenly taller than I remember them. Sonya's smile fades from her face and turns into a smirk. I know that smirk very well. It's the smirk she makes when she's getting ready to make fun of someone. Sometimes the other kids will think it means she's just joking or smiling but this smirk is not her smile. It's not the smile that fills me with warmth watching the way her lips part and cheeks expand up. This smirk fills me with fear. With furrowed eyebrows, Sonya stares into me and closes the space between us as she says it louder this time:

"You like me, you lesbian!"

"You tried to hold Sonya's hand at my house in the dark. I saw it!" Wendy chimes in.

Suddenly, I'm surrounded by snickers that break out into "Ohs" and "Ahs" and "That's so gross, man." Everyone backs away from me quickly yelling out "no one touch her", seconds before the cafeteria doors open. This is the moment I've been marked. Everyone starts to shuffle into the cafeteria around me. They remind me of schooling fish, the way they are trying to avoid coming close to me. Wendy and Sonya stick back to yell out one last thing:

"Don't try to sit with us at lunch. Don't come near us ever again. You're gross and weird."

Sonya's eyes remain on me, her smirk still there until she turns to face Wendy and together they burst out laughing as they run off into the cafeteria with the rest of our grade. I'm left alone in the hallway not sure what to do next. A teacher spots me from the cafeteria and calls me over to join everyone else.

Weeks after, at a family party, it'll be Yasmine who will explain to me what a Lesbian is. She'll tell me briefly in front of my cousins as a way to try and get back at us because we've come together to stop her from bullying us. "Get away from me" she'll shout.

"You're the worst of the worst. That's why in school you are known as The Lesbian. You like other girls. A marimacha. A lesbiana. That's why you don't have any friends. No one wants to be around you. They think you'll try to hold their hand or worse, kiss them!"

My cousins will launch at her after she says this and that's the last we'll see Yasmin. Her parents won't want to come around our family anymore because according to them we're violent and we've got a lesbian in the family.

I spent the rest of the fifth grade playing alone and watching everyone else play together. No more Wendy's, Sonya's or even Yasmin's.

I have thought a lot about why this memory returns to me now. An idea haunts me: Did I do something that night that exposed me? I find myself thinking. With this memory returned I can suddenly feel the sleeping volcano of shame I didn't know I've been carrying with me. How did Wendy and Sonya guess something about me that would take me years to come to terms? Was it the color of my sleeping bag? Lavender is a pretty gay color if you ask me. The way I dressed? Maybe it was the fact that I liked to wear my younger brother's sweatsuits. I pick apart all the superficial things that could have outed me so young as a coping mechanism to avoid waking the volcano of shame. But I feel it start to boil. It was probably something I said or did.

I begin to excavate. To police my ten-year-old self remembering this friendship. In the same way, I recall policing myself around women after I finally came out in college. The shame volcano starts to get hotter when I think about how I've policed my body and actions around other women. The volcano is playing a game with me, the hotter it gets the closer I get to understanding the shame.

I work my way again and again through the pieces of what I can remember of this sleepover:

Did my eyes linger somewhere for too long? When Sonya held my hand that night, did my touch transmit some kind of desire?

The truth is, I think I knew I liked Sonya differently then. I knew there was something about her that set her apart from the other girls for me even if I couldn't really identify what my feelings for her were. Sonya with her big beautiful smile. Sonya with her soft hands. Sonya, who I always wanted to be around because she made me feel warm inside.

I knew I liked to make her laugh and bring her things that made her smile. I didn't know then that the warmth I felt was more than a girl happy to have a friend. A girl doing anything and everything to make another girl smile felt in a way normal to me then. When I was ten, desiring closeness and connection with Sonya only felt like an extension of a special friendship I dreamed of having with another girl. Thinking through all this makes the dormant volcano of shame bubble even more. I'm getting closer to the truth.

I can see the blurred line drawn between the little girl I was, who wasn't fully aware of her feelings for another girl, who seemed to only want a best friend and the adult I am now who understands some of those feelings weren't linked to friendship at all. The full truth is: Sonya was my very first girl crush. The full truth is: Sonya was also my first heartbreak and rejection too. I had swallowed that to protect my ten-year-old self from the belief that this shame is holding on to. The belief that if I admitted to having a crush on Sonya, they were right about me. There was something weird about me.

The way I desired Sonya's kindness and warmth was wrong because it was also linked to a desire for something that made me unlikeable. Something that made others want to avoid me, to pretend I didn't even exist. Remembering all this is making me hyperventilating and spiraling.

Could I be trusted around other women? Is that why female friendships felt so difficult for me? I'm flooded with memories of all the moments this shame and questioning has been affirmed over the years. I'm reminded of what it was like to be a lesbian on an all women's college campus. Straight women I'd meet or befriend urging me that I found them attractive and I needed to confess to crushes I didn't feel or pushing themselves on to me to see if I'd take the bait.

They wanted their attractiveness affirmed at the cost of my identity with no interest in pursuing anything real. Those moments affirmed the fear and shame I developed after that early unconscious attraction I felt towards Sonya and the weight of the rejection, not just from her but from everything else that came with it.

This shame is multi-faced and deeply layered like my skin. The connection comes down to the word Lesbian. The connection comes down to the links I created early on between desire and attraction and shame. It's why when I experienced my first orgasm with a woman, I wasn't rocked by a wave of euphoria but instead hit with a sense of doom. Desire collides with shame, turning them into one another, creating a heavy knot that sits in my stomach and silently reminds me something isn't right about me. I can't be trusted around other women. Emotions becoming mantras on repeat: I desire and I'm weird. I want to and I'm disgusting. I need to and I'm manipulative. I like and I'm a predator.

My wife kissing me on my lips breaks me out of the pool of shame. This shame I couldn't see before. None of that is the full truth. It's different versions of the truth I needed to hold on to, to make it where I am today. I was a ten-year-old girl seeking a meaningful connection. A lonely girl looking for a best friend and I was also a girl with a crush on another girl. One who didn't understand that it's okay to want closeness, admiration and care for other girls and not know exactly when it means something more It's okay not to police your body around other women, to trust yourself. It makes sense to me now why my body now doesn't settle into platonic physical affection from other women. Why doesn't it feel safe and wants to flee it. Part of me is still that wounded little girl who lost a friend because she liked her too much who hated being a girl who liked other girls.

Shame can be dormant this way. Shame is multilayered. I needed this volcano to explode. I need this memory to return. Memory gave me the chance to recognize the shame and uncoil it from desire. To uncoil it from this word that I've learned to embrace and call myself. Lesbian, I say out loud when I look in the mirror. Even though I've learned que me gusta mas dicerlo en español, lesbiana. I've built a home and family with my wife of almost a decade. A wife who is also my best friend. I've found that the two are possible. That lover and friend can exist together. And that I carry with that too, a wounded little girl's shame that still lives on in me somewhere.

But everyday that passes, I feed her wound the closeness I've found with my wife. I feed her wound, memories of my wife and I holding our son's hand as we walk down the street together - Mamá, Mami y él. And I'll continue to feed it the freedom I've felt from loving, being loved and from living my truth every day. But now it will be to purposely, honor that little girl inside of me.

How You Mourn Zara

Chioma Iwunze-Ibiam

I

Is it always the nature of grief to make you wonder, what if? If it isn't, then why do these shelved memories—of the fetus you tried to bury, of the affair with the diver, of the beginning of the unraveling of your marriage to Kene—come unbidden? You aren't sure.

But here you are banishing those memories, pouring them into the mixing bowl, along with the pancake mix, the beaten eggs, the salty liquid that flows unbidden from your eyes. Outside, chirping crickets and ribbiting frogs announce the end of the witching hour. And just as you twist the on-knob of the gas cooker, the crick-ribbit chorus quietens, and the hushed conversations filter in through the gauzy kitchen windows.

Listen to Kene's familiar deep voice muttering, and then to your mother saying, "Go well, Kene. Leave before your wife awakes and flings herself into the toddler's —"

When her final words get swallowed up by Kene's zooming car, resist the urge to plunge the bread knife into your heart. Soliloquize. He's gone to bring Zara home from the antiseptic-smelling freezer truck in which she had been wrongfully entombed alongside other victims of the COVID-19 virus.

Scoop a spoonful of the pancake mix into the heated pan. Listen to the sizzle, pop and fizz of the pan. Hear the sounds as Zara would mimic them. Sizzle, pop, fizz. Imagine her flailing her arms like a polyp in a coral reef, sizzling, popping and fizzing. Imagine her pausing to tuck her oh-so shiny dreadlocks behind her ears.

Flip the pancakes. Perhaps the aroma will travel to wherever they took her and wake her. For isn't she stuck in a dream where she's playing cook with Mama?

She must be.

Just three weeks ago, before she was admitted to the hospital for malarial fever and bronchitis, before she contracted COVID-19 from another patient, before you and Kene were banished into the quarantine center, she had asked, "Mommy, Daddy! Will I help to fry pancakes once I'm well?" And you made her that promise. And so here you are flipping and frying Zara's favorite, well-seasoned with tears.

II

But today, Zara's overpowering smell wafts in with an earthy dawn breeze and moves you out of the house. Not in your nightgown, but in your gray workout gear.

Brisk-walk to keep out the cold. Be blind to the waving neighbors, deaf to their greetings. In your head, Zara sings, "It's cold. It's super cold."

Further down the street is the Blessed Tansi Catholic Church, where Kene often took you and Zara to Mass. Your brand of Protestantism accommodates your husband's Catholicism in a mixed marriage that once transmogrified into what you and Kene termed an "open-mixed marriage." Unsanctioned by the church, of course. Six years ago, after his necrospermia diagnosis, your husband came home with images of men pulled from Facebook and Instagram. "How about this six-packed dude with his glossy skin?" Kene asked.

On another occasion, he said, "Is your handsome account manager back on the market? His relationship status on FB reads, 'it's complicated'" Even when your hands hurt from shoving away his brightly lit MacBook, even when you rolled your eyes and said, "Not my kind of man," and "Not interested," Kene never let up. Your eight-year long marriage was inching towards the tricky ninth anniversary and he was desperate to populate your union with children. It seemed odd for a practicing Roman Catholic who preferred his own company to talk nonstop about "the pros of seeing" other people. He gave a long-winded speech about reducing the feelings of guilt and jealousy by "jumping into those murky waters of the dating scene as a team" and "egging each other on." When you got pregnant, he argued, the baby would "resemble one of us" and the rumormongers would stop speculating about "the emptiness of our childless marriage."

You heard what he was too broken to say: the necrospermia diagnosis wasn't the only motivating factor. His stepbrother had called him an "impotent eunuch" at a family gathering, and though Kene had sucker-punched him, the words stung and filled him with an obsession to prove his virility.

And about a year after you'd rejected Kene's proposition, Constantine reggae-danced into your life. You were thrilled by the novelty and the mystery of the dreadlocked diver. It was around this time that you stopped attending mass at the Blessed Tansi Catholic Church.

And now, here you are brisk-walking past the church's long street, past the Trans-Woji bridge with its waters crashing into rocks, rushing towards the Atlantic Ocean. Stop and look over the railings into the silvery, frothing waves. If you dove into the water, and the tides swept you away this life into an island of coral reefs, would you morph into the kind of mermaid who sinks ships with her singing, the kind who never mourns?

Lift your left leg over the railing. Breathe. Raise the right leg and halt to the strident shouts of "Hey! Hey! Stop! Craze-woman!" And as gravity forces your right leg down on the tarred sidewalk, pull back the left leg. Scan the faces to see who called you a craze-woman. Wipe off the tear trailing down your cheek, shudder at the thought of your body smashing into river rocks, consciousness fading into the ether. Stomp your feet. Jog around the corner. Race past the filling station, past the antique shop with the scratched reef marine aquarium on the display window. Freeze.

Goosebumps wash over your skin as you recall Constantine's living room, the gowned Jizō statue in his coral reef aquarium,the polished brown face and the dimpled wrists of its hands clasped in a prayer pose and Constantine saying, "it's a memorial, a water baby shrine, for my stillborn daughter in London."

Constantine's residual voice goads you through the swinging doors of the antique store, where you lift the aquarium onto the counter. There's no jizo statue. Just two sad-looking tetra fishes swimming in its two and a half gallons of water. Yet you say, " I left my purse at home. Can I take this and bring the payment later today?" The shopkeeper says, of course. You are, after all, one of her regular customers. Hoist the aquarium into your arms. Hurry out of the store.

"Zara, are you near?" You mutter as you trudge past the unfamiliar cars lining your street and crowding your driveway. Only a lunatic will flout the lockdown guidelines to have a pandemic party on a Tuesday morning. Stagger up your oyster shell-bordered walkway.

The door is ajar; swings back when your shoulders nudge it open. Step into the sitting room, hold your breath. Yes, there are relatives, friends and friends of relatives helping themselves to your pancakes. The stainless-steel tray is empty, save for crumbs. You do a headcount. Eighteen people are sitting or standing one meter apart. A social-distance gathering.

Oh, not really. Kene is sitting at the dining table with milk clinging to his mustache, giving it the appearance of graying hair. Perched beside him is Ify, all scarved and gloved and masked in matching print wax material that sets off her glowing olive-complexioned skin. She tugs the sleeves of her off-shoulder blouse and smooths the wrinkles on her bell-bottomed trousers. It's the first time you've seen her since you were pregnant with Zara. As you watch her patting Kene's back with a gloved hand, you find her manner intimate and unpleasant. So you glare at Kene.

You push the aquarium into the hairbreadth of space between Ify and Kene, until the space widens to sit the water container.

“Did you bring Zara home?” you say, beating on Kene’s shoulder as though it is a door you want to crack open.

“She—no, her body—is government property,” he says, holding a saucer of pancakes between you.

“Sue them. What if she’s trying to get out of the body bag?”
“Kasarachi, please stop.”

This isn’t how you expect your daughter’s father to grieve. Cuddling with the ex while Zara is God-knows-where?

Your mother rushes out of the kitchen, mug in left hand, bread knife in right hand, mouth stuffed with pancakes. “Kasarachi,” she says. “Where have you been? Everyone has been trying to offer their condolences.”
You want to say: This is why I detest funerals. Funerals are trouble. Funerals are friends and relatives and friends of relatives gathering to deliberate on the misfortunes of your life.

But before you can mouth these words, mournful faces present themselves. Your mother-in-law overshadows them all with her impossibly high afro, shaped like a mushroom jellyfish. Her boombox voice pipes a notch higher. “Kasarachi, I’m still in shock!”

Shake your head. Say, “Mama, I don’t want to believe this is the end.” Your eyes and cheeks sting from holding back a storm.

Your mother-in-law reaches out to rub your shoulder but lifts her hand to scratch an itch under her afro. “ You’re still young. You can still have another one,” she says.

Think: Why would I want to replace Zara? You have heard your mother-in-law make wicked suggestions to a childless woman. "Marry another wife for your husband," she had said to the other woman as if infertility was the sole preserve of women. "My step-mother paid the dowry for my own mother. That's how she filled her husband's house with babies."

She will not say these things to you, because she is mourning her granddaughter. She loved Zara, bought her educational toys and clothes and body oils. Even now, her wrinkled cheeks are stained with tears.

Lug the aquarium into the master bedroom, place it on your reading table. Secure the locks to the door. If your heart feels heavy with inexplicable grief and longing it's all because you can't nuzzle Zara. You can't kiss her forehead or do the mosquito dance with her. And you think you're being punished again for not burying the first fruit of your womb. And you're curious about the presence hovering above you again, pressing down on the parting on your head.

Open your diary. Start the sentence with 'I.' Cross it out; start with a 'you'. It's easier to frame this narrative from the perspective of your youness. "I" hisses as though your heart is seared with a branding iron.

III

Take four pictures out of Zara's photo album. Brush each photo with the tip of your finger. Linger at the shiny dreadlocks and the stubborn chin that yielded to open-mouthed laughter whenever Kene tickled her ribs. Constantine's dreadlocks. Constantine's chin. Well, it was Zara's bright eyes that Kene proudly showed off at family gatherings, during Mass, at playgrounds. Even now, you can hear Kene and Zara giggling over sweet-nothings and singing nursery rhymes in Igbo. Drop the pictures into the aquarium and watch them sink to the bottom. Then walk away.

Traipse around your four-bedroom flat. Searching the corners of the house, the crevices of your soul. A presence corkscrewing around you the way Zara used to. Yawning in your soul is a Zara-sized hole. Groan. Pace like you did in your off-campus apartment after you had an abortion in that nameless, soulless clinic at Mile 1. You were a twenty-year-old rape survivor, in your second year at the University of Port Harcourt.

Even now, your heart flounders wildly in your chest at the thought of scanning the sunlit, lonely street for the police before waddling through the varnished mahogany door. The receptionist barked at you because your hands shook while you filled the registration forms. You didn't mention that you had slipped misoprostol pills into your cervix and that you had been in active labor for six hours. A cornrow-haired girl chewed gum loudly and complained that you were holding up the line. You apologized and handed her a pen. She couldn't have been more than thirteen. An hour later, she sauntered ahead of you while you waited for your cervix to dilate more.

Soon it was your turn. Your hands shook as you peeled off your underwear and lay on the table, your teeth clenched; the abortionist's-gloved hand slipped into your cervix before you had a chance to wonder about its unsanitariness. But you live in a country where abortions are illegal. It didn't matter if you had died on the table. So you smiled when the doctor announced, "No need for a D&C. Your baby arrived whole". You hoped to leave with the fetus. Better to bury it yourself than to have the quacks sell it to potioneers. But alas, your request was met with a dirty look and a plume of marijuana smoke. For the next two weeks, you cry, bleed and pace in your apartment thinking, *I should have fought to bury my own fetus.*

Nineteen years have elapsed, and yet traipsing around the four-bedroom flat drains you, like regret.

Now, you regret the times you had scolded Zara for turning the house upside down, for putting potatoes and onions in socks and shoes, for breaking the screen on your iPhone, for scream-singing. Kene often said the walls came alive whenever Zara's voice bounced off them. You'll give anything to hear Kene and Zara sing along to a Igbo rhyme or folksong.

Time folds in on itself and the weekend ends with your legs pulsating from the endless pacing. You cannot bring yourself to teach Evolution to your Biology students via Zoom. When you aren't picking at your breakfast on the kitchen counter or forking around your lunch in bed, you sob. For dinner, you eat a bowl of fruit salad in the living room while Kene shakes his boxing glove-sized fists and yells at the people in the News: Lai Mohammed, Trump and Fauci, WHO and the Madagascar government. Scientists are developing a COVID-19 vaccine. Hundreds die in Italy, Spain and the United Kingdom. The Prime Minister of the UK is in intensive care. Hundreds of corpses are packed in refrigerated boxes like Zara.

It takes seven days for the fissures to appear in Kene's fortress. After watching the news, he locks himself inside the guest toilet and weeps. His sobs lull you to sleep on the living room floor. Zara struts towards you in a buttercup-hued sundress. Two jet black ropes of dreadlocks stray from the bun atop her head and dangle in front of her left eye. You croon her name and open your arms wide, inviting her to hug you. She pauses and says, "Why won't you let me go? You have to let me go!" You bolt up in bed, wide awake, drenched in sweat, howling.

Narrate this dream to your husband and your mother and to your sister when she calls from Hong Kong. End each retelling with a cry and an itch to scrub the house with bleach and disinfectant. Launder and pack boxes of toddler clothes, Merriam-Webster's *First Dictionary with Illustrations*, pink toiletry bags and jumbo building blocks set to the Catholic Church orphanage. From the orphanage, drive to the FedEx office to mail Zara's pictures to your sister's hotel room. Don't forget to pay for the aquarium on your way back from the courier's. And while the store clerk counts your change, narrate your dream to her. But resist the temptation to share it on social media. Constantine might be scrolling.

IV

If you hadn't accidentally grabbed his suitcase from the airport baggage reclaim, Constantine wouldn't have taken yours. But it so happened that you'd both wound up at the Port Harcourt International Airport, strange suitcases in hand, trading insults over whose fault it was that you'd both gone home with each other's heavy baggage.

The airport manager claimed responsibility and said he was sorry that the security officers hadn't been around to check the tags. You didn't notice Constantine's stubborn mouth and the umber tips of his dreadlocks until you were both out in the sunlit parking lot, lugging your suitcases in the rain.

When he said, "My apologies. Need a ride?" you ignored him and looked around for a taxi. But the rain had done to the taxi drivers what smoke does to mosquitoes—dispersed them. His offer was your best bet, so you said in your fakest voice, "A lift will be appreciated. Thank you."

He peeled your fingers off the handle. The smoothness of his uncalloused hands made you wonder if he had spent most of his life getting fish spa treatments.

He drove like the oil and gas expatriate that he was, carefully, horn-averse. You wondered if he was one of those black British men who had chauffeurs but didn't like the idea of using their services. Perhaps, he was. You gave him directions until he pulled up beside the giant black gate of your school.

"Is this where you teach Biology?" He asked.

You scratched your cheek and nodded. It was obvious that he had gone through your stuff as much as you his.

"How risky is it to work as a deep-sea diver?" You asked, as you dragged your suitcase out of his boot, out of his life.

Or so you thought. His detailed handwritten letters began arriving at your office; one per day, for thirty working days. Each couriered letter sharing details about his life as a saturation diver and a recovering marine conservationist. Each letter arrived with gifts Londoners like him offered: flowers and water-themed postcards and chocolates. His un-Nigerian love gestures made you laugh and made you shake your head with pity. "Mr. Constantine," you said when you finally called his number. "This is no way to woo a Nigerian woman, certainly not a married one."

But by the end of the phone call, you had consented to meet with him. Constantine had had no qualms being vulnerable with you. You sat on the soft leather couch listening to the regret in Constantine's voice as he discussed his routine as a saturation diver; replacing oil pipes and shoveling mud when he could be discovering what new species were being spawned and which genuses were becoming extinct. "The figures on the paychecks." Constantine kissed his fingers and whistled. "Makes you feel you're kissing working class life goodbye. Blimey, these oil industries offer saturation divers much more than marine biology labs and the National Geographics of the world."

As he talked, you nodded thoughtfully, recognizing the dilemma of being torn between two loves—one wealthy in the capitalist sense, and the other, sublime. You wished you had pursued marine biology too, not settled for biology education; but like Kene, you were averse to displays of penitence, all invocations of repentance.

You could have told Kene about the relationship, but you were uncertain about where this thing with Constantine was going. And there was the excitement that came from the spontaneous meetings and the deception you peddled from the bedroom you shared with Kene to the settee in which you lounged with Constantine. The excitement that came from seeing someone who spoke fluent oceanography and took your mind off a guilt complex you'd been suppressing for years. And it was satisfying to know that Kene hadn't strayed. Yet.

As the days wore on, you blamed your inexplicable yearning for a space to reimagine the possibility of going diving. Of course, you'd been addicted to the adrenaline rush that came from sneaking around.

And on the third night—after Constantine told you about his plans to get a post-doctoral degree in marine conservation—you didn't resist his hungry hands and lips. He'd waited for months since he poured out the contents of your suitcase on his bed. And now that he had you under him, he couldn't help but weep in excitement,"at last! At long last!" Yet, you indulged him. It didn't matter that Kene was more attentive during foreplay, more experienced at lovemaking, and that you were a little distracted when Constantine slid inside you.

Two woofer speakers amplified the snapping and whopping and purring choruses that arose from the bioluminescent coral reef aquarium on his shelf, drawing your attention to the colors. The olive greens and buttercup yellows and mandarin oranges of the floating island no longer shimmered with brightness as they had two weeks earlier, when you first pulled out *Issue 19: Journal on Coral Reef Islands in the 21st Century* from Constantine's bookshelf.

"Bleaching," you murmured.

And Constantine held still and breathed lustily into your ear, "What did you say?"

"The coral reef island. In the aquarium." Brushing the creases above his saucer-wide eyes, you added, "It's bleaching, you know, the rising temperature of—"

"Shhh," he interjected, planting his warm lips on yours. But not for long as your bodies transitioned from the missionary position to a pose that would have been perfectly suited to your thirty-five-year-old body, if it'd been versed in the practice of extreme gymnastics.

You didn't mind because you got a better view of the bleaching coral reef. Like this reef, your marriage with Kene was suffocating. Your eyes locked with the bold stare of the Jizo statue with its ox-blood colored bib and blood red bonnet as Constantine groaned and pulsated inside of you.

V

Kene spends the entire weekend incinerating the serrated-edged kites he constructed with Zara. You shut the windows to keep out the choking smell of burning plastic. But the windows are transparent enough for you to watch the tall flaming tongues leaping into the sky and as you do, you re-imagine Zara palming down the plastic bags, placing the longer raffia broom sticks over the shorter sticks and yelling 't!' because the frame of the kite formed a small letter T. In the last inferno, you hear Zara's squealing embedded in the crackling fire. The squeal she let out as her father carved the plastic bags with his favorite serrated edged bread knife and secured the frame to the plastic bag, and glued two polyethylene tails to the edge of the kite. The squeal gives way to the slap-slap of Zara's running feet and her high-pitched cries of "Flee kite Flee!" The tongues of flames morph into several tiny yellow kites flying against the smoky blue sky. Only God knows how many kites Kene made for her.

As the last of the kites smolder in the garden, you swing around and see Kene eyeing the toy car wash and doll house he'd been planning to surprise her with. You know they will be the next recipient of his rage. And you'll have to rely on the shut windows to shield you from the painful noise of his choked sobs. Even Ify hasn't been spared this silent rage. These days, he ignores her calls. When he picks up, he mumbles monosyllabic responses.

While they are at it, you yawn; too tired to care. All your energy goes into sorting and arranging Zara's photos. One for each passing day. To commemorate the tenth day of Zara's death, you curate ten passport-sized photos and crowd them into the aquarium. One for every kiss Kene gave Zara upon your exit from the delivery ward. Staring at you is a portrait of a grinning Zara, and a bright-eyed Kene—his afro gleaming healthily with eumelanin, his pursed pinkish lips planting a kiss on Zara's cheeks.

Later at night, you lie supine, counting the partitions on the ceiling. Your body yearns for the warmth of another body. You can't explain this sudden need, but the surprise doesn't stop you from tiptoeing down the corridor into Kene's room. Snuggle up to him and kiss his neck. Caress him and whisper, "I need you."

"I'm too tired," he groans sleepily.

Bolt up and pull down his pajamas. "I can help you with that."

Outside, two thunderbolts roar.

"No." He pulls up his shorts. Fat rain drops drum on the pane of glass. "I'm not in the right frame of mind."

You think: he's no longer attracted to me. Perhaps he wants a second wife. Perhaps he wants a spouse who will never come home smelling of another man's Jamaican peppersoup pot, or another man's cum. Your mind conjures up a vision of a younger wife, sashaying in and out of the rooms of your four bedroom flat, swinging brandy-hued braids that brush against her large buttocks.

Unbidden tears roll down your cheeks and slide onto his unshaven chin. His bare shoulders shudder. Plant a kiss on his clavicle. But resist the urge to let your lips linger. One kiss is enough to comfort him through one night of grief. Wipe the rest of your tears with the back of your hand. Storm out of his room.

VI

In your room, the reflection of a lightning bolt flashes across your bed. The lazy rumble of thunder precedes the persistent drumming of fat rain drops. The music puts you in mind of that rainy night four and a half years ago, when your marriage faded into a bone-whiteness.

You remember walking through your living room door, tossing your key on your center table and hugging Kene from behind. He sniffed. Perhaps at the earthy, garlicky scallions or the nutty, bitter callaloo on your breath. Then he turned to face you. Down rolled the flame-shaped okra he had been slicing with the sharp bread knife.

"What did you have for dinner?" he asked, in a tone so playful, it made you put down your guards.

"Jamaican peppersoup pot," you blurted out, picking up the green okra.

His lips stretched into a mock smile; his hands gripped the wooden handle of the bread knife. "At the PTA meeting?"

"No." The staple refreshments at PTA meetings were meat pies and Fanta, not Jamaican cuisine.

Sniffing again, he said, "I can smell him on you."

Your eyes latched onto the knife in his hand. Why was it so easy to extricate the right answers from you? Perhaps, it was his skill as a lawyer or it was the knife in his quivering hand. Or perhaps it was the exhaustion from all the gymnastics of the oh-so slow lovemaking at Constantine's. So you leaned against the wall, biding your time as he pontificated about the benign and malignant types of adultery, and open relationships like the armchair theorist that he was. When you couldn't bear it any longer, you interjected:

"So it took me one year to—"

"Take advantage of the situation?"

Up in arms, you shouted: "You wanted an open marriage!"

"For children, yes." Sighing he added, "You said, 'not interested.'"

"That's not fair," you cried. "It was your idea."

"Is that the most convincing excuse you can come up with?"

The words gushed forth through Kene's clenched teeth, the white lights from the fluorescent tubes glinting off the serrated edges of the bread knife. Fear made your tongue a leaden spoon in your mouth. The lazy rumble of thunder floated in through the window, into the space between you and him.

Although you had wanted to, you couldn't say that there wasn't a mutual exclusivity between his supposition and your decision to sleep with Constantine. And you couldn't bring yourself to say that you hadn't adulterated anything. In fact, there was no stock of pure breeds to spoil. But you knew his ego was bruised and that he couldn't be blamed for having necrotic sperm cells. So you clamped your lips shut.

Kene charged and roared and knocked a whole basin of okras to the floor, his breath rising from his chest in noisy heaves. More light bounced off the serrated edges of the knife and glinted in his wet eyes.

"Why hide the whole koko from me?" he cried. "It's the lies and betrayal that hurts."

"But, I didn't think you'd want to know!"

The refrigerator chugged; the power went out. Fumbling for your phone in your handbag, you bit the bottom of your lip to keep from howling. The LED lights on your phone cast a glow on his receding shadow as it stormed down the corridor into the guestroom.

"Kene?" The flashlight on your phone came on. "Wait."

He held up the bread knife. "Don't you dare come close."

Slamming the door behind him, he snapped the bolts, turned the locks twice. You kicked the door and growled and roared. You tried to pack your things. It was easy to fold your clothes into your suitcase, but your best photographs were his too. Dividing them down the middle would ruin them so you left them and picked up the towel that smelled of his Old Spice shaving cream and the Gucci sandals he bought the previous year, when you turned thirty-five. Ring finger in your mouth, you bit your wedding band and slid it onto your tongue. Its stinging metallic tang smarted your cheeks, until you crouched and broke into choking sobs.

It was in this squatting pose that you sent Constantine a text message. You don't remember the exact wording of the message, but you do know that it was harsh and insincere, and that as you blocked his number, rivulets of tears rolled down your cheeks.

When the neighbor's rooster crowed the next morning, you went to the guest room door and called his name. No answer. The sliver of space underneath the door revealed moving feet, which you watched as you listened to the sounds of his heavy breathing.

You left a tray of food and jars of water on the dining table. But when you came home from work the bread had hardened from exposure, the runny eggs spotted three dead houseflies; the milk in the beverage curdled on the edges of the teacup. And the door stayed locked.

The following day, you peered through the sliver of space underneath the door, saw his barefooted pacing, heard his heavy breathing, and decided to leave the tray of food and water in front of the guestroom, where a bump from the door would have spilled some of the soup and water. And as you taught pupils about life forms and living things, you imagined a cloaked, hunchbacked death skulking along the corridors of your home, pitchfork in hand. What if you came home and found that Kene had stabbed himself to death with the serrated bread knife?

The pungent smell of rotting fruit salads, soured soups and moldy garri hit you as you unlocked the living room door after work. Tiptoeing to the guest room door, you listened to the sounds of breathing, and pissing and cracking knuckles. Eyes raised to the heavens, you muttered, "At least, you're alive."

On the third day, you awoke to the loud whistling of the pressure pot. Your first thought was burglary. Tiptoeing down the hallway to the guest room door, you rapped on the door and said, "Please Kene, there's a burglar in the kitchen."

Silence.

"Please, come out and help."

The banging of pans drew you to the kitchen. Through the keyhole, you could see an unshaven man march around the kitchen like the man you had been married to for nine years. A slight push, and the door yawned open to reveal a stone-faced Kene stirring a pot of reddish-brown beans and plantain porridge. You slapped your hand over your mouth to keep from screaming about his jet-black hair suddenly turning gray.

And so, you awoke each morning, thinking you'd stay, just one more day, in your section of the four bedrooms even when Ify the girlfriend sashayed into your lives, first visiting one rainy weekend from Etche, fiddling with your turntable, whistling to the tune of some obscure music, swinging brandy-hued braids that graze her large buttocks. You stood transfixed at the door saying, 'who are you? why are you here?' Tracy Chapman's voice boomed from the stereo as Ify swung around and said, "I'm Ify, Kene's girlfriend." Kene waltzed in, a bottle of Hennesey in hand, only freezing when his eyes met yours. How long did you stand there glaring at each other? One minute that stretched into a millennia? Perhaps not. But you do know that as you clenched and unclenched your fist, that you wanted to punch him in the mouth and to rip off Ify's bum shorts.

But all you did was storm into your section of the house while Ify traipsed around the flat swinging her voluptuous hips. Even when you could hear Ify shrieking with delight from the caverns of the guest room. Even as you developed a heightened sense of smell that turned your stomach every time she sauntered past your door and left a trail of citrus. You stayed and soliloquized about staying just one more day in this house, with this man you once thought you could never live without.

But this was the era of nonsensical happenings, when you were always on the chancy side of statistics. According to an HSBC study, there's a one in fifty chance of finding a romantic partner on an airplane. You did. Also, there's a 30% chance of conceiving in your first month of trying. When you heard this from your gynecologist, you never thought it would happen to you.

Also, you never envisaged that Kene would be so excited by the news that he would abandon Ify in the guest room, and cross the invisible barricades to say, "sorry, ndo" while you retched into the toilet. You were shocked when he smiled at the bump on your stomach and said, "Kaka, you're pregnant." Shocked because you'd been in denial, because you'd been ignoring each other for twelve weeks since Constantine

Yet, you nodded and whispered, "yes." even though you hadn't expected

Kene to say, "Let's get you to an antenatal clinic."

VII

A post lockdown Monday morning. The room smells of Peak 123 milk and rain. Slivers of dawn light streak through the curtains. Wear regular teacher's clothes—a beige suit, dangling earrings and sensible leather shoes.

As you stride through the tree-lined entrance of the government school, keep your chin up. You've worked here as a Biology teacher and a guidance counselor for eight years, but you've never felt so empty, so inadequate, so lost. Not even when Constantine sent you his last postcard, the one that read, "Hello Kay Love, I'm sorry to see you go."

Sit in your wood-partitioned office, and wait for teenagers to waltz in and say, "Ms. Kasarachi, will there be a second wave of the pandemic?" Or "Are we experiencing the apocalypse? Or, am I in love?"

Hand out flyers absent-mindedly. Acknowledge the emptiness in your soul. The Zara-sized hole.

During break, while the kids play football and basketball, screaming their heads off, the school Principal walks in and says, "Kasarachi, kedu? I hope you're stronger."

Nod. And say, "Good afternoon. Sit."

"No. no. I won't be here for too long," The school principal says.

Think: like Zara. But say, “Okay.”

When she says, “Sorry for your loss.” Flash a tight smile that says; can you believe it? — *I just lost my baby. I don't know where to find her. I know where her body is, but she's no longer in it.*

Exhale. Then say, “If I could fight God, I would. Anyi a ga aba Chukwu ogu?”

The Principal nods like an agama lizard. “Have you heard of urine therapy?” She says, shifting her weight from one leg to the other.

“Urine therapy?”

She nods and her voice goes down a notch. “You know it cures convulsions and viral infections in children. My first son convulsed when he was eighteen months, and on my mother's advice, I forced my urine down his throat.”

Clear your throat. Say, wide-eyed: “Were you crazy, really?” Then palliate that rudeness by saying, “Sorry, urine stopped the convulsion?” “It worked like magic.” She snaps her fingers. “At least it worked for me. And I heard some COVID-19 patients recovered after they'd tried a combination of herbs and urine therapy.”

On your way home from work, ask Kene if he has heard of urine therapy. Don't ask him if his mother fed him piss.

He furrows his brows. “Urine what?”

“Therapy.” Repeat the school principal words. Talk with your hands over your head.

"I don't understand a word you've just said."

Sigh. Tell him to take you to the movies; it won't be a super-spreader event. All moviegoers will have to sit and watch from driveways and parking lots.

At the movies, he'll caress your arm and kiss your shoulder. Fill your mouth with popcorn and stare at the screen. Try to remember the title of the movie or why you chose it.

"Excuse me." His sexy baritone whisper will startle you. "Off to the gents. I'll be back in a jiffy."

Go with him. Admire the way his jeans cling to his flat bum. Take in the turned up collar of his Arsenal T-shirt and his oversized moccasins. When he comes out wiping his hands on his jeans, don't slap his bum. Say, "You boyish man! Where's my lawyer husband?"

"He's still mourning so he asked me to show you some fun."

Lean into him. Pour all your grief and frustration and hopes into the kiss. Let the tears roll down your cheek and then, push him gently away. Back at home, bid him good night and sashay into your bedroom alone. Sigh. You know what all good teachers know: pedagogy is fifty percent acting.

And acting, like mourning, is all about feeling.

VIII

You're lying in bed daydreaming of fat-legged babies pirouetting in tutus atop an aquarium. Zara's voice booms out from behind a series of swiveling doors. "Let me go," she says, in a quieter, more matter-of-fact voice. "I have to go."

Your eyes flutter open. Yellow bars of noon sunlight fall atop the aquarium; its disintegrating pictures swirl like strange underwater creatures. The door swings open and your sister saunters into the room dressed in a flowing ankara gown, smelling sweetly of citrus. "Ginika!" you say, as if you hadn't heard she'd flown back after the border had reopened. You act surprised for her sake. Gnika likes to surprise you, like FedExing you the exact kind of brandy-filled boxes of chocolate Constantine bought when he was wooing you. But your sister doesn't know anything about Constantine and she is eager to hug you, eager to say, "Kasarachi, I'm sure you have heard enough sorrys to last you five reincarnations."

Hum softly when she makes small talk. But when she throws a protective arm over your shoulder and says, "Quick. Get dressed. We're going to Freedom Stadium for a gospel concert."

Brush off her arm, say, "Concert? With social distancing?"

Ginika flashes a smile. "Tickets and snacks are on me."

Skip lunch and dinner so your stomach won't bulge through your favorite silk shirt Ginika bought you. It's a ChiJesu and Ebelebe concert. A pair of jeans and a shirt will be perfect.

The stadium is packed full of masked and gloved fans. Each person has a vacant seat to their left and right. Ginika flashes your VVIP tickets and you slide into second row seats with the creme de la creme of the Niger Delta.

Thank Ginika for the cup of juice and roasted meat she hands you. Empty the cup in three quick gulps. Near the retractable roof of the stadium, a bevy of ladies are singing, through surgical masks, at the top of their lungs while rocking on their feet.

"The year D and I moved to Holland, we had a child who died." Ginika bows her head as though in a prayer. "A son."

Stare at her with mouth agape.

"I didn't know that," you say, after the rocking ladies stop singing a chorus. "Did mummy know too?"

"I was too depressed to disclose the birth of the baby. Let alone his death. I forbade D from telling anyone."

Ginika closes her eyes. "He came prematurely. At seven months. Was alive and suckling for three days. And just when I got used to keeping awake at night and all, he just went puff!"

Stab a piece of meat with your toothpick, mutter. ""Oh my God." You don't know what else to say, because you would never dismiss your loss as something that happened thirteen years ago. You would never say, "I don't dwell on it too much" because you aren't like Ginika. .

With a gentle squeeze of her hand, try to rekindle a kinship spirit.

"But how—"

"Shush." Ginika points to the stage and you sigh, feeling absolved of the guilt of hiding your abortion from her.

Onstage, ChiJesu is plunking a soulful symphony on his piano. Ebelebe is strumming his guitar. The atmosphere is charged with singing and swaying. Sometimes, you sing whatever song they are playing. Sometimes, you drift down memory lane, conjuring long sleepless nights spent nursing, changing diapers, cuddling, and chatting in babynese. For some reason, your mind flashes images of the near cot death, Zara's mouth foaming with breast milk; a pajamaed Kene driving her to Briggs Pediatrics Hospital.

When the tears start flowing, don't wipe them away. Stand and sing in an angry voice, then hum songs of salvation, and of un-disappointing hope. Shiver under the weight of the lyrics, at once pressing down on your chest and lifting off your grief in slow portions.

A cold hand tugs at your outstretched hand. It's Ebelebe, guitar slung across his shoulder blinking tears from his eyes. He says: "Come. Dance upstage." The cold from his hands grip yours.

Shake your head no. Sway to the new tune ChiJesu plays, your favorite, Zara's favorite, *Forsake Me Not, Lord.*

"Go on, you dry woman," Ginka mouths, her head bobbing slightly.

Walk upstage with Ebelebe. Step gingerly as though you might slip on the wet grass and fall. Yes, God has forsaken you. Throw your hands apart and twirl like you saw Zara do in front of the TV once. Call up memories of dances with Zara, of plans to register her in an elite ballet class. Swing, glide and step back. Your sorrows won't fly away but swing your arms and twirl. It's all you have now, a grand chance to let go, to soar like a bird, with your heart hanging hollow. Ebelebe catches you to steady you. When ChiJesu plays the coda, remember the hopelessness of that cold, dingy abortion clinic; the blindsiding pains you trapped within you as a yellow cab drove you to your dormitory.

Twirl. Think: Does Zara dance with that nameless baby? What's this life worth? Dear God, at least music moves you, shakes the foundations of your being like an earthquake. Fall on your knees. Your life is not your own.

IX

At home, Kene shuts the door behind you and says, "How did it go?" Grin at him and walk into the guest room. Say: "Hmmm Ebelebe was so impressed, he gave me his jacket. See?"

"I can see. But please tell me if you decide to start seeing him."
Slip out of your sweat-drenched clothes. Say: "That's an expensive joke."

"You started it!"

He charges into his room, rolls onto the king-sized bed, muttering something about wanting to sleep in peace.

Jump on top of him. Say, "You want to sleep in peace? Or you no longer want to stay married? ."

"Kasarachi, what's wrong with you? Listen," The air conditioning hums noisily and he holds your hands apart so your faces are so close, you can feel his warm minty breath on your face. Angry and warm. "What do you really want?"

Take in the lines around his tired eyes. Sigh, say, "Kene, I had an abortion when I was eighteen." Pause to take in his wincing noises. The vent of the air conditioner grunts and heaves like an old man. "And when we were having problems conceiving, I thought we were being punished for something I'd done."

His grip slackens around your fingers.

Sit up, say, "Each time I got my period, I felt like a hodgepodge of barren organs." Let the tears roll down your cheeks and drop on his unshaven chin.

But it's not the abortion that you regret; you couldn't have done otherwise. You just wish you had buried the twenty-week-old fetus. You don't have the words to explain this conviction. Also, part of you fears he'll judge you for yearning to bury your dead babies, for wanting to get closure.

So you let him stare at you, his eyebrows arched; corrugated lines etched on his forehead.

When sweat begins to pool under your arms, roll on to the bed and say,

"It's okay if you decide to quit the marriage for good."

Outside, a neighbor's dog growls and whimpers. Kene clears his throat.

"Kasarachi, our marriage died when Zara died,"

A strong wind rattles the blinds, slips into the room through the chinks in the windowpanes. Goosebumps cover your skin, not from the cold, but from the dread of abandonment. And yet, you look straight into his eyes and dare him to divorce you.

"But," Kene says slowly, "but we can start over if you want."

Cry. Say: "Why? You don't even bloody love me!"

"Of course, I bloody love you. Do you want me to shout from the top of Mount Kilimanjaro?" He bear-hugs you and grabs a chunk of your hair, until your wig comes off.

Your lunch of spiced roasted meat and juice slowly make their way up from your gut onto your throat. Hurry into the toilet and retch. When Kene comes in, let him hold back your hair while you empty your gut.

"We can start over," you say, "But I won't share you with anyone."

Just as you look up from the toilet bowl, he pulls the lever on the water cistern, and says, "Likewise."

Wipe your mouth with a paper towel. Say: "Really? And what about Ify? Is your breakup final?"

It's almost midnight; not a good time to open the ex-files. And yet,

Kene indulges you, says:

"What about her?"

"What. About. Her?"

The water cistern quietens. All you can hear is your pounding heart, his heavy breathing.

"Kasarachi, I don't want her. If I did, I wouldn't be here."

Saunter off to your room, leave the door ajar. Don't cry in excitement as he drags his pillow, his toothbrush and his box of underwear into the master bedroom you once shared.

X

A windy Monday morning. Cumulus clouds block the sun. Move the aquarium to the living room to make room for Kene's bags.

Drive to work. Avoid the Principal. Offer walnuts to the students who come for counseling. Shift papers around the office desk until the closing bell rings.

Drive to the flea market, humming gratefully for the calm of the post-lockdown, rain cooled atmosphere. On the drive back home, you see a long-limbed dreadlocked man at the tail of Miniokoro bridge handing over a wad of notes to a roadside artist. Slam on your breaks and reverse your car, looking out the window to take in the silky kinkiness of his dreadlocks, his oily ebony-complexioned face. His long, strong diver's arms lift three sheathed paintings into the backseat of the SUV whose lavender scented seats you remember so well. Is It Really Constantine? Four and a half years have passed since you last saw him, but you'll recognize those umber locs, anywhere. That stubborn chin, too. It's him all right, albeit with a rounder tummy. Yet still here, unaware that he fathered a child who died a month ago. He deserves to know about Zara, you think as your car turns full circle at Rumuobiakani roundabout. You can just tell him and be done with it.

Park your car on the Miniokoro Bridge, a few feet in front of him. Hop out of your car and watch Constantine slamming shut the back door and opening the driver's door. Your eyes lock. For two seconds. You're sure because your heart skips two beats. You open your mouth to speak to this man who is both familiar and unfamiliar to you. Staring into his eyes, you feel a weight on your chest, like the morning Zara was buried. What you want more than anything is to feel his diver's arms around you; to hear him promise to make a water baby shrine for Zara. But he just stares at you, perplexed. Look down at his leather shoes. Wince from the pain of yearning for things you can never have.

Hop into your car and drive homewards, peeking into your rearview mirror to watch him scratch the worry lines on his brow. His mouth hangs agape and for a moment, you wonder if he's howling your name. But your name doesn't start with an 'O', you think as you watch his poised, unconstrained figure grow smaller and smaller, narrowing into a dot that disappears when you swerve into Woji Junction. As your car halts at the legendary Woji traffic, bang your forehead on the steering wheel until the traffic eases up and your car accelerates past the redundant train track. How naïve of you to think that a conversation about the three-and-a-half-year-old Zara would roll off your tongues as easily as your discussion about coral reef triangles and deep-sea diving and water baby shrines?

Nothing will prepare you for the sight of Zara's school bus parked beside the house. Clean your eyes to be doubly sure you hadn't imagined Constantine on that Miniokoro bridge and that you aren't, in fact, imagining the proprietress and the tiny pre-school children who have accompanied her to your home.

Squirt sanitizer onto your hands. Think: *Oh God, they're too young to be paying condolences.*

Your husband has served the loaf of Madeira cake from the fridge. And oh, Kene served zobo juice from the freezer. Grab the bread knife from the tray and cut yourself a wedge.

Sit and place your cake on Kene's saucer. When the proprietress perches beside you and holds your hand, inhale the lavender fragrance of her expensive perfume and smile politely. The first day she met Zara, she had said: "Bright eyes. Can she model for BC International School? Her beautiful face will light up the school's billboard." The picture is on a billboard somewhere on Port Harcourt city's expressway, but you haven't seen it. You never will. Now, the proprietress says, "Is it okay? Do you want us to take it down?" And you shake your head and say, "No, don't. Zara will like it up there."

Stand up when the kids finish their food. Listen to them croon *Abide with me* in an off-key fashion. It takes you a while to make out the tune. Sway gently, sing along and think, life's journey is confusing as hell, but full of new beginnings. There's no fight left in you and your sorrows are forgotten bundles scattered about the abandoned battlefield of life. Savor your husband's breath on your neck as he leans behind and holds you, his voice blending nicely with the children's. Smile. Remember: every reef is shaped by the waves and storms and heat it encounters. Acknowledge that you will never get over this loss, and that you don't have to.

Altar Server

Lauren Francis-Sharma

The Sunday that thirteen-year-old Patrina heard the news about Alejandro, she was selling Kool-Aid icee cups from her kitchen door. Her new sign read TWENTY cents a Cup, wich was now five cents cheaper than her latest rival's, Poppa. Patrina always took note of the traitors who walked the alley dropping paper bits of Poppa's cheap Dixie-cupped icees like breadcrumbs, and Michael was one such traitor. She'd seen him on his way to Poppa's bouncing a basketball shoulder-high, and now he shoved a spoon of what looked to be a cherry-flavored icee into his mouth.

"Oh, I see how you do. You gonna eat the competition's icee right in front of me?" Half-joking, Patrina pointed her finger at Michael as she ran toward the end of the white picket fence.

Michael was wearing his usual Orioles cap low over his eyes. He grinned, then glanced down at Patrina's bare feet, at her unpolished toes and the heels peeling white.

"I was coming by to check on you," he said. "But I see you're your usual loud-ass self. Go on inside and put some cocoa butter on them ashy legs, and on your way, get me a pink lemonade." Michael chuckled and moved up the concrete walk, slowing only to take note of something in

Patrina's mother's azalea bushes.

Michael, nearly four years older than Patrina and halfway through high school, was thick and muscled by that early June day of 1986. He wore a bleached white tank as if it were skin and a wave cap beneath his hat that masked the full bushiness of the sideburns he'd grown since last summer. Once, he had been part of the St. Phillip's Catholic School crew who convened in basements, dancing and playing board games. As the leader of the crew, Michael had taught them the Hustle, he'd taught them how to pop wheelies on the Big Hill, how to play dodgeball with particular cruelty, and most memorably, how to French kiss. Everyone had a crush of some sort on Michael and Patrina had been halfway through fifth grade when she begged God to let Michael demonstrate a French kiss on her, but he had always treated her like a little kid, which only worsened after he mysteriously left St. Phillip's, pulling away from their crew so that they only saw him on occasional weekend afternoons.

But now, suddenly, he was in her backyard.

"Your mother home?" Michael's left eyebrow arched and Patrina wanted to believe his question suggested an interest in spending private time with her, but she soon remembered the last time he'd been at her home, when her mother told Michael never to return.

It was a month earlier. A group of them had signed up for the Hands Across America charity event that everyone in the country had been buzzing about. Her mother had promised to drive them to their designated spot in the D.C. suburbs. They were all so excited to be a part of a human chain that would extend from the east coast to the west coast, maybe even with the chance to be on television. But Father Gilbert called just as Michael and Alejandro, Patrina's best friend, gathered on Patrina's front porch. Father Gilbert needed two altar servers for the eleven o'clock mass. Some of the long-standing servers, older boys whose families had long ago left the city in the second round of white flight from Baltimore, had called out sick, and though Patrina didn't think this was her problem, her mother, a staunch West Indian Catholic, proud that Patrina was the first girl to serve in the church, stood at the storm door with the phone cord stretching from the kitchen, and told Father Gilbert that Patrina and Alejandro would skip Hands Across America.

"Aww man," Alejandro whined.

"Your mother's a bitch," Michael whispered.

In their neighborhood, no one could call another person's mother that word without repercussions. Alejandro's eyes widened, as he uttered an "oooooooh" that was so long and so instigating that Patrina couldn't possibly let it pass. As her mother said goodbye to Father Gilbert and as Michael readied to leave to search for another ride, Patrina told her mother what Michael had said.

"Yuh betta not let me see yuh blasted face at my house again!" her mother shouted at him. "Yuh have problems wi yu head?! Someting is very very wrong wi yuh!"

The moment she heard her mother's Trinidadian accent emerge so distinctly and so loudly, Patrina regretted telling on Michael. Even old Ms. Beverly, who often remained in bed twenty-hours a day, peeped through her blinds to see about the commotion. During mass, Alejandro berated her for what she'd done, told her she would never live the betrayal down, but now Patrina had the chance to make it all right with Michael. She'd have to sacrifice her body but it would be worth it.

"You wanna come inside?" She licked her top lip the way the white girls did in the Nair commercials.

Michael scoffed, the sound like a shovel on dry concrete. "Lil girl, you'll get your feelings hurt if you walk around offering it up like that. Just go on and get me that pink lemonade."

She was both humiliated and relieved by his rejection and watched as he mindlessly reached into his pocket for a quarter, staring out again at the azaleas. Someone had thrown the tire from her old tree swing into the bushes and ran off with the manila rope. Patrina, thinking little of his far-off expression or the missing rope, hurried into the kitchen. She shoved aside the ground beef, chicken thighs, the pack of broccoli, slamming ice trays, until finally she had to confess.

"I sold the last pink lemonade to Alejandro. You want grape?"

Michael jumped from the rail and snatched open the storm door.

"When was he here?"

"Who?"

"Alejandro."

"I don't know…yesterday or the day before. Maybe it was yesterday. I also have watermelon. You want watermelon?"

It was, in fact, two days earlier, on Friday, when she and Alejandro had walked home from school on the last day. They'd had a quick meeting with Father Gilbert who wanted to discuss the summer's mass schedule. Being the newest altar servers, the two of them always had the last pick of Sundays but now with so many of the other boys quitting, Father Gilbert offered them first choice.

"We gotta get our summer plans together," she'd said excitedly to Alejandro. "We should take only the 12:30 masses, right?"

Alejandro, usually talkative, said nothing until they neared home. "I'm not doing nothing this Sunday" he said. She agreed they'd skip Sunday. Then, Alejandro asked if he could have the last of her pink lemonade icee-cups. "Please?"

"I bet you ain't even got a quarter." She laughed and Alejandro emptied his bookbag onto the sidewalk. Two dimes plunged to the concrete, along with test papers he'd clearly hidden from his parents. There were Fs on all of them. He had always been an A/B student.

Patrina didn't take his money. She never had, never would because Alejandro was her closest friend. At their age, they weren't safe to admit this for surely he would be called a faggot by the other boys, while her father might sneer and pretend he wasn't intimating that she was a slut. And their nightly phone calls, which they both pretended was about homework rather than about *Family Ties* and *Miami Vice*, would be put to an end.

Now, Michael lowered his voice, nodding toward Alejandro's house.

"I thought you were just trying to be tough, but you don't know, do you?" he said.

"Know what?"

In that Northeast Baltimore neighborhood, stories wended their way through back screen doors, through mesh wires not tight enough to withstand the gust of whispers bedded between *you didn't hear this from me* and *they'll kill me if they knew I told you*. Patrina leaned in, the anticipation making her almost breathless. What did Michael know that she didn't? Her eight-year friendship with Alejandro had been formed out of their perceived difference. They were the only two children of foreigners in a southern-rooted American neighborhood. Their parents cooked with coconut milk and with beans that were not green and fried things their friends mistook for bananas. They ate spices, the smells of which wafted out of alley-facing metal vents where playmates stood questioning both their palates (*that shit can't taste good*) and their hygiene (*all that garlic stays in your skin*). Living in America, Patrina and Alejandro's families, though from very different places, seemed more like the same kind of different. When Alejandro's dad in his wife-beater, took up his machete to trim weeds, Patrina was reminded that her father stored his cutlass in the basement storage closet, taking it out only to hack at green coconuts bought from the Chinese grocer.

Looking at Michael's brow collapse now, Patrina imagined that Alejandro had gotten into trouble again, that his mother had had to miss work for a last-day-of-school meeting with a roundtable of teachers who couldn't understand what had gotten into Alejandro as of late. Or that Alejandro's father, who'd lost a whole hand in Vietnam, had again chased him out into their backyard.

"Alejandro's father's at it again, huh?" Patrina said.

"He died, P. He died on Friday night."

Patrina felt her shoulders falling, felt her bottom lip loosen. Alejandro would be heartbroken. Though he had had a fraught relationship with his dad, the loss would be unbearable, for there'd always been the hope that one day things would be different between them. Thinking of it now, Patrina remembered seeing Alejandro crying in the cloak room, then she'd seen Father Gilbert holding his hand in the vestibule of the church after school. But on their walks home, Alejandro never mentioned that his father was ill and, in fact, he'd denied that he'd been crying, denied that Father Gilbert had ever been clasping his fingers.

"How'd he die?" Patrina said this in the same way she'd heard her mother react to the news of any unexpected death. Her mother always wanted to know *the how*. Then, she would sit with the news for a few longish moments, before emitting what to Patrina felt like canned utterances. If it were cancer, she would always say *Damn cancer*. And if it was a heart attack *At least he went quick*. And for accidents, her mother became much more philosophical. *Every day is a blessing but it can all be gone in the blink of an eye.*

"Killed himself," Michael said, as he stood between the door and its frame.

"Noooo."

Patrina had never seen her mother react to news of a suicide. She, herself, had only heard of one person, a young man from the county who'd been mentioned on the 6 o'clock news. He'd been playing with his father's gun. Had that been a suicide? She didn't know.

Michael handed Patrina his threadbare Dixie cup and his masticated wooden spoon, gesturing for her to do him the favor and rid him of the burden of carrying it. A fly flew in over Michael's head and Patrina, worried that her mother would be angry, urged Michael to come inside, but Michael, instead, released the storm door and stood on her back porch. The wham rattled the foil-covered grates on the stove.

"Have you seen him?" Patrina spoke to Michael through the screen in the door but she was thinking of the plans she'd made with Alejandro to take the bus to the skating rink later that night. The rink had a School-is-Closed Sunday night skate special and at lunch on the last day of school, everyone had agreed to meet there. Alejandro would probably not want to come. Who would she couple-skate with if he stayed home?

"We won't see him until the funeral, I guess," Michael said.

Geez, Alejandro would have to reconcile this loss with what they'd been taught about suicide being a sin. God will forgive everything but that, Father Gilbert had told them. Patrina wondered if Father Gilbert would perform the rites for Alejandro's dad, wondered if he would mention what he'd told them in class.

"Do you think God really won't forgive you for suicide?" Alejandro asked her on their way home from school that day.

"It makes sense." Patrina had shrugged. "I mean, you can't go to confession after you do it and you can't promise God you won't do it again."

Alejandro had nodded.

Now, Michael climbed atop the porch rail once more, looking in the direction of Alejandro's house. Past the Smith's rose trellis and the Harris's clothesline, Patrina wondered what Michael could see.

"All that blue." Michael shook his head. "My mother said that wasn't a good color for a house."

A few months earlier, Alejandro's uncles had painted their traditional, Baltimore, red-brick home, a bright robin's egg blue. Alejandro had told Patrina that he felt like he lived in a "barrio," and that the color brought too many eyes. She didn't have the heart to tell him he was right, that everyone in the neighborhood hated it, that it brought unwanted attention to her foreign family too.

"I know you and him was kinda close," Michael said now.

Patrina wanted to tell Michael that she hardly knew Alejandro's dad, but she thought it'd be rude. He'd once taken a bunch of them to Wildwood, New Jersey and sat on a wooden bench while they rode the rides. Sometimes, before Sunday mass, while helping Alejandro to brush back strands of his hair, Father Gilbert would ask Alejandro about his uncles and his father. Alejandro's face would tighten and Patrina would nudge Alejandro to remind him to behave. They were the only altar servers from seventh grade, and Patrina knew they'd be treated as outsiders if they didn't make nice. Father Gilbert had tried to bring Alejandro into the clique of boys, taking him to baseball games and watching movies at the rectory, but Alejandro complained that Father Gilbert was too nosey.

"He should mind his business. And what's his obsession with my dad? He's always asking people about their fathers."

"Maybe he's trying to make everybody's father come to church more." Patrina had laughed.

"My dad hates church and he hates that he calls me *Alex*. He told Father Gilbert I can only serve two masses a month and they had to be with you."

"With me?"

"He wants to make sure I come straight home after mass, and you always come straight back home."

Patrina had felt embarrassed by her do-gooder reputation. It was true that she had done nothing extraordinary with her adolescence. No cigarettes, no peeking at *Hustlers*, no cherry-popping. Just Atari, and the occasional sneak to watch *The Golden Girls*, which her mother called smut. She was predictable, boring, childish, so much so that apparently Alejandro's dad entrusted his only son with her. How humiliating.

"You think I should call him?" Patrina asked Michael now. The fly performed a pirouette before clinging to the door's mesh. It stared at her.

"Or maybe I should go knock on the door?" she added.

Michael turned his attention to the tire weighing down the azaleas and to the poplar tree beside it. She imagined he might've been thinking of the times they'd all raced to the top limbs. Michael, much bigger, always made it up first, pelting them with sticks and fighting them off with branches as they neared him. Once, when Patrina and Alejandro were seven or eight, Alejandro earned a handsome cut on his cheek during the climb. Michael had been frightened of getting into trouble with Alejandro's dad. When Alejandro ran home, they watched from the bottom of the alley as he came across his father inside the old Ford he liked to work on, but Alejandro ran straight past the old car and into the house. When he returned outside, his cheek dressed in a Band-Aid, Alejandro's father promptly exited the car and ripped off the bandage.

"I heard his pops is all torn up." Michael twirled the hairs in his adolescent moustache and Patrina cocked her head as if trying to hear Michael better, but the fly's buzzing distracted her. It seemed a plea for her to pry open the door.

"Alejandro's father's pops is all torn up? Alejandro's grandfather? I thought his grandpas were both dead."

Michael glared at her, his head tilting before he covered his mouth. He jumped off the rail, told her to come onto the porch. The fly wailed, confused, as it tried to squeeze through the opening alongside Patrina. It didn't manage a clean exit, so it watched her from inside.

"Alejandro, P. Not his dad." Michael spoke slowly. "Alejandro is dead. Alejandro killed himself on Friday night. Hung himself in the basement."

Patrina squinted. "You said Alejandro's dad."

"No, no, I didn't. You just thought that."

"But we're going skating tonight. He didn't call to tell me he couldn't go."

Patrina looked again to the rubber tire, while Michael assured her that he had the information right. At a time like this, her mother might've clutched her chest or even gasped. Should she do that too when what she really felt was the urge to vomit? Michael reached for her, his hands under her arms, holding them aloft as if she were a scarecrow. He had a strange look on his face as if he could feel her heart thumping through her chest, as if he could feel how warm she suddenly grew. Patrina, trying to focus on something, looked down at his left hand. There were faint scars across his wrist. He was a rough-n-tumble boy. Scars from sawing lumber for go-karts and diving across the alley's concrete surface would be expected. But the scars at both of Michael's wrists were neat, precise, not the kind he'd earned from climbing a chain link fence. Michael pulled her into him now, hugging her as the fly's buzzing ceased, replaced by the sound of clinking metal.

"Michael, you must have plenty better places to be." Patrina's mother stood with her keys in hand, her figure darkened by the screen's netting, her perfume catching in the air, an admixture of rose water and Youth Dew. Michael stepped away from Patrina.

"Patrina, where's de meat I ask you to soak in de sink? What we eatin' for dinner? And what's this fly doing in here, Patrina? Michael, gimme a minute, I wanta talk to you." Her mother spoke quickly, the sentences blurring, as if from one breath. She set her bags down then joined them on the back porch. There wasn't enough space for the three of them on the landing, so Patrina turned to leave, thinking only of Alejandro. Was he really dead? Was he Pac-Man dead or like old people dead?

Inside, Patrina spotted four cartons of eggs in the grocery bag her mother had set on the kitchen floor. In their neighborhood, death brought a certain efficiency. Baltimore hadn't yet been ravaged by crack cocaine and the city was still brimming with Black folks who bore big country hearts and big country ways. After news spread of a death, neighbors would brine pork, order flowers, clear parking spaces. And Patrina's mother always made deviled eggs. Alejandro had been dead for two days and the eggs seemed like confirmation.

"You knew?" Patrina muttered.

The fly buzzed near Patrina's left ear, as her mother, on the back porch with Michael, squared her shoulders, her expression suggesting that she was not the kind of woman who would question whether she'd done right by her daughter. Patrina lamented that she had spent most of the weekend happily on her Atari, thinking not one minute about Alejandro since he'd left her on Friday.

Well...that wasn't exactly true.

While playing Pitfall, Patrina *had* thought about calling Alejandro to play, but she knew he would beat her, and she also knew his dad would say he had chores to finish. Alejandro had always been scared of his dad.

The day after the Hands Across America, which had been all over the news for failing to achieve its goal, Father Gilbert, acting as their substitute math teacher, told them that no organization other than a church could get that many people to show up at the same time to hold hands with strangers. "A waste of time," Father Gilbert had told them. And that's when Alejandro blew a raspberry. Father Gilbert punished him by locking him in the cloakroom after school. Of course, the principal, Sister Elizabeth had already told Alejandro's parents that one more reprimand would lead to a suspension, so when Alejandro didn't come out of detention after an hour, Patrina thought it must have gotten pretty serious. The next day when she asked Alejandro if he'd gotten into real trouble, he told her that Father Gilbert had let him off with a warning.

"But he's telling your father, right?"

"No."

"Stop lying!"

"He said it was our secret. He wouldn't tell my pops so long as I obey him from now on. I can't get in trouble with my dad no more."

Patrina reached for a kitchen towel to hunt the fly now. She would wait until later to ask her mother what she knew about Alejandro. Maybe the eggs were for someone else? Then, the phone rang, and by the way her mother scurried inside to answer it, Patrina knew it was something or someone important.

"Oh yes, I was expecting your call. " *Long pause.* "Yes. I'm sure." *Longer pause.* Oh, she would appreciate that."

Her mother held the phone out toward her. "Take it," she whispered.

"Why didn't you tell me about—"

"Shhh…" Her mother pushed the receiver into her chest.

"Hullo." Patrina's tone was flat, achy. She didn't want to talk to anyone, not until she knew for sure what was going on with Alejandro. "Yes,

Father."

Michael tapped the metal lower half of the storm door as Father Gilbert was saying something about the importance of appreciating pleasant weather.

"Sorry about everything, P. If you make more pink lemonade, let me know." Michael waved at her. "Bye, Ms. Castle."

"Michael, wait, I want to ask you something else!" Patrina's mother moved quickly through the door and down the walk. Patrina watched as her mother leaned toward Michael, his mouth downturning, his head shaking in a *no-no-no-no-no*..

Meanwhile, on the phone, Father Gilbert cleared his throat. "By now, I'm sure you've heard...I know how much Alex meant to you. He meant so much to so many. But you had a special friendship. His mother would like to know if he told---"

"He didn't say anything."

"Many people don't. It's a terrible thing."

It must be true, then. Father Gilbert wouldn't call unless it was true.

"I should have known."

Father Gilbert fell silent. Patrina hadn't expected his silence.

"The funeral will be on Tuesday. I would like you to serve that day. Alex would want that."

She wanted to say no. If she'd been the dead one, she wouldn't have wanted Alejandro to stuff himself inside a heavy robe to give people wine and biscuits. She wanted to be in the pew with her parents, not with Father Gilbert who'd be pretending he didn't believe Alejandro was going straight to hell.

When her mother returned inside, her brow was pleated, like the heavy drapes she'd made Patrina iron every Spring. She cut the meat out of its pack. Frozen ground beef sizzled in the pan, as her mother stared at the phone.

"What did Father Gilbert say?"

"You already know. You practically told him yes before I had a choice."
"Watch your mouth." Her mother took the towel from Patrina's shoulder and threw it into the sink. "Did it sound like he was surprised about Alejandro?"

"Why didn't you tell me? He was my friend."

Her mother stabbed the ground beef with a fork. "Did Alejandro ever say anything to you about Father Gilbert?"

"What about Father Gilbert?"

Her mother shook her head, much the same as Michael. "Nothing," she said. "I just heard Alejandro's dad didn't want Father Gilbert to do the service. That's all. That's all," she said again, then she sighed.

The day of the funeral, Patrina's kitten heel broke off while climbing into her father's Chevy Malibu. Her mother ran inside, returned with a pair of her own leather flats, a size too small. As Patrina walked the center aisle of the church, ahead of Father Gilbert who held the Bible overhead, her toes felt pinched. This was a good thing, she thought. Focusing on anything but this funeral was a good thing. She needed not to absorb the grief of the mourners, the parents whose eyes seemed to scream *there but for the grace of God go I*, the emptiness in her classmates' expressions. She remembered how, until only recently, Alejandro had been shorter than her, how he'd shot up four inches and gained twenty pounds between Thanksgiving and New Year's. His uniform pants had begun to look so absurd on him. In the early Spring, Michael had invited him to play basketball at the square. He gave Alejandro proper-fitting shorts to wear, and some other St. Phillip's graduates were there too. Alejandro told Patrina that Father Gilbert drove by them in his church car and Michael gave Father Gilbert the finger and they'd all laughed. Alejandro said that Michael told him that when he left St. Phillip's, Father Gilbert banned him for life, not just from the school grounds but from the church grounds too.

"Did you know Michael used to be an altar server?"

Patrina had tried to remember if she'd ever seen Michael serving mass.

"He said Father Gilbert asked for too much."

Patrina rolled her eyes. "Father probably wouldn't let him listen to The Fat Boys on the boombox in the rectory."

Alejandro asked her what sin she thought Michael could have committed that Father Gilbert would expel him from church. She said she didn't know. Then, he told Patrina that Michael had given him a few puffs of reefer.

"Michael said it would make me forget things, but it makes me feel like I could jump from the top of the monkey bars and take off flying." Alejandro grinned. He told her he wanted more.

"Michael was wrong to give you that."

Alejandro called her "Granny" and waved her away. It was the first time she felt like she was losing his friendship.

Now, the organist played the selections Alejandro's mother had requested. The musical notes from the balcony echoed between the shuffling of mourners. She spotted all her classmates and a few of the elder neighbors who attended all the funerals, including Alejandro's grandmother, who was seated beside Alejandro's mother, who was the sort of Catholic who hung rosary beads on the rearview mirror of her car, the kind who lit candles and incense when a day went awry. Her short legs, thinly veiled with sheer black pantyhose, were crossed toward the casket. She stared at it as if expecting it to move, while Alejandro's dad, two seats away, sat anchored by his brothers, the house painters, one of whom would read from the Book of Wisdom, moments later,

The righteous, though they die early, will be at rest.

Alejandro's uncle wore a double-breasted suit. He pulled at it while he read from the lined paper. The podium seemed small before him. He was a big man, twice the size of Alejandro's thin, soccer-playing, dad. He adjusted the microphone, which released a stuttered screech, and covered his mouth as if the noise had come from him. Some of the mourners, including Patrina's mother smiled, while Father Gilbert, seated on the throne-like chair, tucked his hands into the wide pockets of his robe, breathing deeply. Alejandro's uncle nodded at Alejandro's dad before he read on.

For old age is not honored for length of time nor measured by number of years...

Patrina searched the pews. People held leather-bound hymnals on benches that were so overfilled that some were forced to sit forward, breathing over the backsides of those ahead of them. And there were a number of people propped against the stone walls. It was cool inside, the thirty-foot ceiling aiding the case, but Patrina knew by the time service ended, they'd all be roasting. "The heat of the mourning," Father Gilbert liked to call it. She wondered about Alejandro, wondered about the air inside his shiny white casket. Father Gilbert had advised his mother not to display the body so there had been no procession, no ability to ensure that Alejandro was in there, except, of course, by his absence. She liked to believe that she and Alejandro had shared nearly everything except for this death.

But understanding is grey hair for anyone, and a blameless life is ripe old age.

Alejandro's uncle slowed, his accent so thick that perhaps he felt he needed to attend to each word.

For the fascination of wickedness obscures what is good, and roving desire perverts the innocent mind.

In the back pew, Patrina spotted Michael, the only Black face in that row, the holy water fount just over his left shoulder, his navy-blue suit too tight across his chest. She was surprised she hadn't seen him earlier, surprised she hadn't noticed his searing expression. Beside him sat a boy named Randy, an eighth-grade altar server, a freckled-face white boy who wiped sweat from his brow. Next to Randy, a long stretch of scowling boys whom Alejandro had played basketball with at the square, all of them white, all of them former altar servers. None of the boys were seated with a parent, and at the end of their pew remained an empty space, a gap the congregants had, for some reason, refused to close.

Being perfected in a short time, they fulfilled long years…

In the rectory, before the service, Father Gilbert, washing his hands over the marble sink, had warned Patrina that funerals for the young were "terribly emotional." He told her she should prepare herself for a more vocal grief, prepare herself for the unexpected. And yet, as she stood at the front of the church, the silence that lay in the air between Alejandro's coffin and the mourners, was far worse than any vocalized grief. This death felt like a silent crushing weight on a chest that felt too insubstantial, too underdeveloped, to bear it.

For their souls were pleasing to the Lord, therefore he took them quickly from the midst of wickedness.

After the reading, Father Gilbert said kind words about "Alex," words that didn't match Alejandro at all. Pious and quiet and obedient and wanting. Words absent the affection Patrina had seen Father Gilbert exhibit for Alejandro. Was Father Gilbert angry with him? She'd hoped Father Gilbert might mention the things she told him about Alejandro--the comical way he trotted down steps, three at a time gripping the handrail with both hands, or the way he loosed his body when he danced or rode his bike with his arms outstretched, or perhaps even the way he tented his fingers when he begged for Patrina's icee-cups--but Father Gilbert said none of that.

As Father Gilbert waited for the congregants to wish each other peace and as Patrina held up the heavy gold-trimmed Bible for Father Gilbert to read from, she turned quickly to glance again at the back pew. For some reason, the boy Randy was now standing. He turned to Michael, who stood too, and suddenly the row of boys were all standing, glaring up at the altar, gripping each other's hands, the last of them holding something aloft that Patrina couldn't quite make out. As she wondered what was happening, she lost focus on the mass. Father Gilbert, noticing, stepped on her pinched toe to revive her attention. Wincing in pain, Patrina dropped the Bible.

"Lord Jesus!" she heard her mother gasp.

The deafening clatter startled the entire church. She reached down to retrieve the Bible, but it was too heavy to lift without a full squat. Father Gilbert bent down beside her, trying to wrench it from her grip, but Patrina held firm, insisting on righting the wrong, searching for the pages he had flagged earlier in the rectory. Matthew was it? But it was Isaiah that opened before her, the words underlined. Had Father Gilbert underlined the words for this service or another? *Of whom were you worried and fearful, when you lied, and did not remember Me nor give Me a thought?*

She pointed to the page as if to ask him if she'd found the correct passage. Father Gilbert covered the mic with his hand. "Stupid girl," he whispered.

Patrina flushed with shame, then suddenly, she felt herself growing angry.

"His name is Alejandro. Say Alejandro." She whispered this only to realize that Father Gilbert's mic, clipped to his robe, was no longer covered by his hand. The congregants heard her as clearly as if she'd whispered Alejandro's name in each of their ears.

Father Gilbert snatched the Bible as the crowd stirred. The mourners were now focusing on the back of the church where the boys had begun to move toward the center aisle. The few non-Catholics, unfamiliar with the rituals, stood to mimic them, while Patrina's bangs blew across her forehead, for Father Gilbert was urgently flipping the Bible's pages.

"We ask for patience and forbearance," Father Gilbert said.

Alejandro's mother, nestled against the corner of the pew, emitted something that sounded like a deep growl, an utterance so primal that Patrina felt tears flooding her eyes.

"Oh no no no no no, " she cried.

Decades later when detectives from the Northeast precinct joined other law enforcement officials to question the congregants of the Archdiocese of Baltimore, they would find a note in a detective's file---lined notebook paper—detailing a phone call made by a little girl from Baltimore city in the summer of 1986.

The girl had questions about a priest..

Northeast Baltimore??? Afro-American girl??? Priest???

Someone at the precinct had written question marks in the margins of the note. A note that would have been entered into evidence except t no one ever followed up with the girl, no one ever followed up with the woman the little girl grew to be.

It was only after the Vatican shuddered under accusations of its criminality and cover-ups, that the folks who'd been in church the day of Alejandro's funeral, finally wondered aloud what those boys had meant to do that day. Moving into the middle aisle of the church like that? Threading a manila rope between their fingers like that? Disturbing that "little Spanish boy's" funeral like that? They remembered Alejandro's parents had packed up their blue house within months, they remembered how the row of boys who'd shouted at the priest had been asked not to return to St. Phillip's , they remembered that the island people's daughter had been expelled from school for turning off the priest's microphone during the service, but no one remembered the name of the priest, the priest who'd been transferred to what he referred to at his last 12:30pm mass, as "a more obedient congregation."

Sworn Virgin

Mauricio Ruiz

When she looked down at her husband the downpour had become a drizzle. Oltana didn't know how to feel. She looked at the burns near his temple, the grey clothes that he wore every day, that seemed to have changed very little in color after he was struck by lightning.

The smell of burnt skin made her numb, disoriented, she knew she ought to be in shock. She felt the heaviness of her clothes, a light breeze making her shiver; she realized it was getting late. She felt her nipples hardened and crossed her arms, the way she used to do when Lazrim entered their room without knocking. Then she looked at the clouds overhead, horses and cherubs and full-bellied dwarfs, they seemed to be smiling at her. She felt the rain in her face, droplets pattering on her forehead, a trickle of water dripping down her chin.

After a moment she murmured to the sky: How did you know that's what I wanted? There was one, maybe two lightning flashes in the distance, then she felt the power of it, the force of nature reverberating through her body.

She rolled her hair to one side and squeezed it, saw the falling drops distort the surface of the puddle near her feet. The earth had become darker, ready to be pregnant with life; she could smell clay and mule dung in the air. She decided to walk home and change her clothes, maybe eat a slice of rye bread before going to visit her sister.

With Lenka she would cook chicken gizzards and boiled cabbage, the stuffed peppers both of them liked, then she'd tell her how it'd happened, the miracle she'd been granted, because that's what Lenka would also do, share her problems and worries with Oltana, the moments of frail intimacy with her husband Mihal, the insecurities that seemed to plague every Albanian man.

Oltana knew what would happen when she informed the elders about Lazrim's death, the way they'd decide how she should be feeling, the words of insincere affection and pity, the unfelt grief followed by the orders. The sacrifice that would be expected of her.

The house where she lived had been built by her paternal grandfather, then inherited by her father, who had kept a room in it until his death. That was part of the agreement with Lazrim: her father could live with them but Lazrim would make all the decisions. The house would be owned by Lazrim and Oltana's son, who would arrive in due time, when God chose to bless their marriage.

Walking down the hill, she stopped for a moment, hands on her waist, and admired the tree that stood a few feet away from the house, a towering elm that had always given her peace, its branches brushing against the brown-tiled roof. When they were children, she and Lenka had felt blessed to grow up near the tree, especially on hot summer days when it extended its branches over them like a biblical giant. In the evenings they had lain on the grass and smelled the fragrant wind of the night, eyes closed, and listened to the secrets whispered by the swinging branches. Both sisters had spoken to the tree, expressed their gratitude and laid gifts around it, mounds of sugar and wooden toys, the tree's ancient roots surfacing like the arms of a mystical creature. Standing in the doorway their mother had watched them, cross-armed and smiling, and Oltana knew she was refraining from calling them in for bed, because she and her sister were in another world.

Oltana walked over and embraced the tree, put her ear on the bark. She felt the rugged surface against the skin of her jaw and earlobe, she stroked herself against it. (what did the tree feel like against her body, her ear?) She smiled and murmured something, words of affection. She sometimes thought it could feel Oltana's heartbeat, perceive her emotions; it knew of her sorrows and joys, held memories of when she and Lenka were little. The tree had witnessed Oltana's father's childhood, her grandparents' and great-grandparents' too, generations of men and women plowing these lands. She pressed her lips to the bark.

Then she felt something, a vibration that came from the center of the tree and entered her body. She took a step back and looked at the branches. She heard a twig snap and turned her head; she felt an odd panic when she saw a man staring at her.

"Are you in love with a tree?"

She noticed the dark bluish stubble, the worn out beret that lay tipped forward on his head and close to his eyebrows.

"You're all wet," he said.

"Do I know you?" she asked.

"I've seen you before. You and your sister."

She noticed the way his eyes were examining her body. She stooped her shoulders, crossed her arms and hid her breasts.

Theatening? Menacing? Creepy?

"Lazrim," she yelled, and raised her arm.

The man turned around.

"Lazrim," she repeated.

"Maybe you know my husband?" she asked, then yelled again. "That's him, over there."

Far in the distance, the figure of a horse could be seen, someone riding on its back.

The man gave her one last stare, then walked into the forest.

She began to run towards the silhouette riding the horse but then thought no. It was safer to go towards her sister's house. She thought of what lay ahead, the men that the elders would present to her as suitors, the face of infinite gratitude she would have to show them. She was a widow now. She stopped and leaned forward, rested her hands on her knees. She closed her eyes. What if she chose something else?

She arrived at Lenka's house and knocked on the door. She turned her head and gazed at the landscape behind her, the young pines up the hill, the missing stones in the path; her footsteps were visible in the mud. A shiver ran up her spine; her throat hurt when she swallowed. She was about to knock again when the door creaked open and Lenka appeared in the doorway, her baby girl in her arms.

Lenka laughed a little, then covered her mouth with three fingers. "Were you rolling around in the mud like a hog?"

Lenka was holding the baby with both arms, twisted her torso to one side, then the other, and Curlina babbled something.

"I don't know where to begin," Oltana said as she leaned forward to kiss the baby on the crown. She smiled and thought of hugging her sister but her body was cold, her clothes wet; she did not want to touch the baby like that. She crossed her arms and cupped her elbows with her hands.

"Are you just going to stand there?" said Lenka. "Come on in."

In the kitchen Lenka put water to boil, waited for her sister to put on dry clothes. She was carrying Curlina close to her chest. The baby giggled and reached out with her hands, she tried to grab Lenka's hair in a fist.

Oltana shuffled into the kitchen wearing an oversized white gown. "Can I help with anything?" she asked. "Where's Mihal?"

Lenka touched her sister's hair. "It's not dry yet. Let me go get another towel. You must be cold," she said, and removed a strand of hair from her eyes. "Do you want some tea?"

"Lazrim's dead."

There was silence.

After a moment Lenka cleared her throat, then said in a low soft voice, "Do you want to tell me what happened? I'm beginning to worry."

"I can't say I'm innocent."

Lenka gasped. "What have you done?"

"Doesn't matter, I've made up my mind. I'll take the oath."

Lenka frowned.

"I'll be free," Oltana went on. "I'll do whatever I want."

"You'll what? No, wait," Lenka paused, examining her sister's face. "Where is he now? Please tell me you didn't –"

"He was hit by a stroke of lightning."

Lenka sat back in her chair.

"I'll take the oath and become a burrnesha," Oltana went on. "I don't care, I want the kind of life they have." She leaned over the table. "That way I'll be able to keep the house and you can come over, any time. Mihal will think twice before getting drunk now." She placed her hand over Lenka's and held it. "The way we always dreamed of."

"The house," Lenka repeated, she was smiling.

"We could lose it otherwise."

"But what about – "

"I don't care about the vows," Oltana said. "What? You think I'll miss it? I never felt anything with Lazrim." She tilted her head and pursed her lips. "I used to stare at the ceiling," she went on. "I looked for the spider knitting its web. Then he was done."

"There are other men. Different men."

"Only Dad was different." She was shaking her head. "Thanks but no thanks, I'm not interested."

"What about children?"

"Children," Oltana repeated, then fell silent. She kept watching a spot on the floor. She did not seem to blink.

After a moment Lenka stood up and touched her sister on the shoulder. "Are you hungry?" she asked. "There's some pork with squash and green tomatoes, I know you love that. No, you sit. I'll get it for you."

Oltana sat cross-legged on the old kitchen chair, half-listening to what her sister was saying about Mihal and the trip he'd made to the city. She was thinking of the days to come, of the ceremony where she'd become a Sworn Virgin and receive the rights of a man. She wondered if it could be possible, that life. She could start smoking, even drink alcohol; she could do anything. Her life was about to change. She felt thrilled and excited and worried. What if it was not what she envisioned? There are other men, Lenka had said. Different men. What about children, her sister had asked. She did not want to think about any of that because she'd be able to keep the family's house. She and her sister, living close to nature. She imagined herself with Lenka and Curlina seated under the old elm tree, eating a watermelon.

After she finished eating the stew, Lenka asked if she wanted to help bathe the baby.

Oltana rolled up her sleeves. "Let's do it."

They heated some water, then carried two full buckets to the small wooden hut that served as a bathroom outside. They poured the water into a wooden tub and Lenka touched it with her fingers. "It's ready," she said.

"No, it's too hot," said Oltana. "Let me stir it a little more."

They sat Curlina on one side of the tub, Lenka holding her back and neck.

"Look at that tummy," said Oltana. "I just want to squeeze it."

"Do you know who she reminds me of at that age?"

Oltana laughed. "Yeah, right."

Curlina kicked the water and Oltana shrieked, moved back but the front of her clothes got splashed. "Not again," she said, smiling. "I just changed clothes."

A knock on the door was heard, first timid, then louder.

"Hold her," said Lenka, then walked to the door.

Over her shoulder, Oltana saw a woman, doubled over and with a cataract in one eye. She was murmuring something.

"I won't be long," Lenka said to Oltana.

She bathed Curlina with care, feeling the softness of her skin, and she talked back when Curlina babbled and giggled; she seemed to have plenty of things to say. They played for a while, spilling more water, Oltana squeezing the sponge over Curlina's head. She noticed the water was not as warm and worried the baby could catch cold. Just a little longer, she kept telling herself.

When she put Curlina to bed, Oltana tucked the blanket under her chin. She looked at her hands, rosy and half-clenched, showing at the edge of the blanket. She listened to Curlina's breathing, fast and irregular, and wondered if she'd ever regret her choice. She bent over and pressed her lips to the baby's head, filled her lungs with her scent.

Downstairs she found Lenka washing the dishes. "What did the woman want?" asked Oltana.

Lenka stopped for a moment, then continued washing.

"Something's wrong?" Oltana insisted.

"Half of the roof fell down," she said. "The other caught fire."

Oltana brought a hand to her mouth.

"Her son and grandchildren are safe," Lenka went on. "But her husband has burns on the back and shoulders."

"Will he be all right?"

"It will take him weeks to recover."

"What about the house? Do they have somewhere to live?"

Lenka was drying her hands with a cloth. "She's just grateful her husband survived," Lenka said.

Oltana looked down at her lap. They were silent for a moment, then Lenka said, "Let's go upstairs."

That night it rained again, with thunder and lightning, but in her sleep Oltana didn't hear any of it. In earliest morning she woke up rested, bright sunlight pouring in through the thin white curtains. She found her sister in the kitchen feeding the baby.

"Coffee?" Lenka asked.

Oltana nodded, then sat at the table. She blew over her cup but did not drink. "I need to go and talk to the elders," she said.

"This early?"

"It's important, didn't you say so?" She stood up. "I'll tell them everything."

Lenka nodded, then walked with her to the door. Curlina held a wooden spoon in her hand and was waving it in the air; she brought it to her mouth in one quick movement.

At the door Oltana hugged her sister. After they let go of their embrace, Curlina giggled and Lenka squeezed her sister's hand lightly, rubbed it with her thumb. "It's not too late," she said.

They regarded one another for a long moment. Then Lenka said, "Whatever you choose, it doesn't matter. I'm here for you."

Oltana bent over and kissed Curlina's head, then walked away.

Outside the air was dry and cold. Scattered white clouds mottled the sky; they seemed to be drifting away without hurry. A breeze from the west stroked Oltana's cheeks, her forehead. She thought of what the elders would ask, the reasons she'd have to give, all of them rehearsed in her mind. She recited the words she'd have to pronounce. Yes, I do. The river meandered and narrowed, then disappeared from view.

She convinced herself it was for the best. Lenka would have more children, beautiful all of them, and Oltana would be there to raise them, love them as if they were her own. She looked at the river once more. Let's go. She walked on the stone path again.

Not far from her house an odor pricked her nostrils, a smell of burnt wood that made her feel dizzy; a slight pain above her stomach began to jab at her. She walked faster, her pace almost becoming frantic. When she saw the old tree, cracked through the middle and charred, she felt as if the air had been removed from her lungs, a shattering of membranes and ripping of organs. It deafened her. She looked up at the clouds and tried to scream but couldn't.

She gazed at her house, unharmed by the storm, then at the tree, at the branches that now lay on the ground, some of them still crackling. She let herself fall to the ground and felt the pain in her knees, the rocks cutting her skin, and she gave a small cry, a muted howl of the soul. In the distance, purple grey clouds were moving beyond the mountains. The sky was turning blue.

Below the Clouds

Yessica Martinez

The day the DREAM Act failed - no graduation caps went up into the air - a caravan - we packed the senate chamber - but we couldn't talk - we were shut up - from the Bronx - I met a girl - who lives two degrees of separation from Prince Royce - this friend cursed out Jeff Sessions - outdoors - a small man under a small umbrella - we kicked the snow - said let's go home - under our caps - those migrant roofs below the clouds

Interview with Diana Khoi Nguyen

Angie Cruz

In Fall 2023 I had the pleasure to speak to Diana Khoi Nguyen about her work and learn more about her creative genealogies.

Angie Cruz (AC): So when I asked you about a work that is part of your creative genealogy you shared: *Lana Turner: A Journal of Poetry and Opinion*. So the question I want to open with is: What does it mean to be in a proto revolutionary moment, one of urgency, anxiety and uncertainty? What does it mean to be in conversation with the left wing avant garde?

Diana Khoi Nguyen (DKN): This text is from 2012, but it's one that I return to because Cal Bedient was my mentor when I was an undergrad. Whenever I don't know what to do in regards to writing, especially when I have an existential crisis, I reread that interview and I ask myself, what does Cal want, as in: what poetry does Cal want in the world? It's not just that the writing has to be experimental, but it's more like, what is the capacity for what one can do. I think about that and it helps me to try stuff I wouldn't normally try.

I don't feel like I'm as political as *Lana Turner*. But I wonder, how could I write something that's political for me that they would call political too? It's my touchstone. I went to Columbia for my MFA and I studied with somebody the opposite of Cal. When Lucie Brock-Broido liked a poem, she drew a unicorn. That's how you knew that she really loved the poem. Like you never saw Lucie when the sun was out, you didn't know what size her body was because her clothes were voluminous. Inside her house, it was all red velvet. I spent a lot of time with her. And she loved a high, lyrical beauty in poem, and also liked truth. Duende.

I shared that interview because after my MFA, I kept writing poems with my mentors in mind. But then I was like, Why do I care what Lucie or Cal thinks? After graduating, I finally asked, what does Diana want? I knew I was political, but I just didn't know how. I needed to find a middle ground: I needed to not be in any one place but to find my own place.

This is a roundabout way of answering the question about that interview. I do agree with this notion of challenging language. It's so hard to make stuff new without it being a gimmick. Because I write every six months, I'm regularly like, "I don't know what to do." And then I go back and I read the interview, try not to email Cal, to ask him to tell me to do something, like give me a prompt because sometimes he does. So yeah, I turn to *Lana Turner* also because there is all this other political stuff in there–yes, capitalism is dangerous, but I'm not sure I want to articulate that in a poem. I don't understand all of the journal's work, but it excites me and it gets me to want to create. Like how the best kind of reading makes you want to go home and explode shit, not literally make bombs, but to try wild stuff on the page. Stuff that feel incendiary.

AC: I am very excited to know that there is literary journal that publishes works that compels us to want to throw the journal across the room.

DKN: Yes.

AC: And that is resistance. To publish work that explodes something in us, in how we see the world. It makes me think of your poem, "Triptych" from your beautiful poetry collection, *Ghost Of* where you say, "do not simply resist, resist; we who are free to move around who are free, bewilder, we bewilder what we fill in what bewilders us to fill in what" When I read the word bewilder, I heard Be wilder.

DKN: I love that. Be wilder.

AC: Teresita Fernandez, a Cuban visual artist, was asked, "what is your aesthetic?" And she said, "well, aesthetic. Is this just awareness? The definition of the root of aesthetic is to be fully aware." So my question is, when did you find your aesthetic?

DKN: That "Triptych" poem you mention was the first one I did. I'd gone to sleep the night before, rereading that *Lana Turner* interview, distressed, thinking I'll never write again. I can't write anything that is helpful. So the next day I asked myself, what am I not talking about? I mean, I'm a person who's very transparent. I'll share everything with you. But even so, there's still things I'm avoiding. For instance: I couldn't look at these pictures that were still hanging in my family's house. They're fucking scary. I had to ask my sister to scan and send them to me. And when you scan stuff and then put it in a Word document it's ginormous. But it wasn't so scary when I opened the file up because it could be zoomed on somebody's shoe. A 1994 shoe is a lot less scary than a portrait of a family with a brother cut out of it. And then I slowly began to zoom out. Then I could hold it. When it became overwhelming I would move to another part of the picture.

This may not be writing, But this is still part of the practice. This is a big part of my practice even now, even when I don't work with an image within a piece.

Think about what's on your desk when you're writing, authors, the books, what objects, what's at the altar, the desk. I literally push it as a watermark in the page, like I'm writing over ancestors and I just remove the image later. It's like writing with ghosts. They're there to second guess: what are their stories and what do I remember about them or what I do not know about them. I now welcome the practice of Tina Campt, whose work I love. She has a book where she's working primarily with images within the Black diaspora, *Listening to Images*. It's auto-ethnographic. She talks about how images emit a frequency that we cannot hear but we can feel. Like sound waves! For example, my voice right now is only disappearing and people can't hear it outside because all your bodies, the carpet, the walls, the wood, the concrete is absorbing that sound. The image, which is seemingly inert, is also emitting. It's communicating to us in some way and sometimes we can pick up on it. And when we can, what are we going to do with what we feel? This is another way of asking what draws you to a particular visual element and what do I have to say about it? A lot of times it's not necessarily drastic in describing what I'm feeling, but sometimes to the ghosts and ancestors I sense around me, I'm like, "Hey guys, come on in. Let's type together." The writing becomes collaborative, it's also a family, also a diasporic documentary. Writing at first made me feel uncomfortable. I couldn't look at the images my brother left behind until a year after this death. I hadn't cried since I got the phone call that he died. I didn't cry at the funeral because it all felt so was weird. I didn't have access to how I felt. The images scared me. So I had to break down the scary thing into tasks: for example, putting a text box over the dead brother's white cutout space and filling it in with text–the cutout space determining the line breaks. After doing that, I realized I had much more to say. So I asked myself, what if poetry or what if creative writing could be a framework around the person who no longer exists? Then I wrote over the photograph and around the cutout space, text hugging the void. As I did that, I started crying, and it seemed that the floodgates opened up from inside. I had no idea that would happen. That white space was a key hole which unlocked pent-up emotions from over a year. When I consciously and intentionally decided to stay and write in the cutout space, it gave me access to all these things I didn't yet know how to engage with.

Family documents give me access to more of myself and other parts of family narratives. I continue to collaborate with images. I often wonder, what else can photographs unlock for me? Before, I used to hope that a poem would arrive, especially during grad school; often I'd hope for a good dream the night before a poem deadline.

Now, I'll make a gardening analogy because I'm currently working to remove the monocrop sod in my backyard. I want to plant native and indigenous plants so that bees and butterflies native to the region can come, eat, and thrive. But I'd like to do that with my imagination too. What other books can I nourish it with? During the writing of *Ghost Of*, I fertilized my imagination with materials around the theme of dust. I watched movies, read scientific papers, nonfiction, fiction, things that I wouldn't normally pick up, and consumed materials that were both tangentially or directly related to dust. I took notes, but also wasn't trying to directly write about dust. This fodder gave me access to metaphors, similes, and diction that I wouldn't normally have. This approach continues to give me a way to continue being a student long after I've graduated. This is all part of my aesthetic now: how can I continue to pollinate and fertilize whatever this patch of earth is (that is my brain)?. What new crop do I want to plant and how might I prepare the field for it? There's a lot of labor involved in preparation. Sometimes I don't know what it is I need to say, but I can give myself a foraging basket and use the foraged words and images to begin to put stuff down. The writing process is one of much preparation, and one of unending discovery.

AC: It's not that different from my creative process. I spent many, many months waiting for inspiration. As I'm listening to you, I'm thinking about that moment when one is fully aware of the thing that unlocks creativity. I like to be invited to do things that are outside my wheelhouse because, I'll try something I don't know a lot about and think, it's okay if I fail miserably, at least I tried at something. Can you tell me more about the ways that you collaborate and work anonymously with your collective?

DKN: I'm part of this female and non-binary Vietnamese diasporic artist collective called She Who Has No Master(s). The work we make doesn't have an author. The author is the collective, but everybody contributes to it. It's not just: I (as an individual) am gonna write something. And it's also not an exquisite corpse. The collective shared document is amorphous and sometimes filled with chaos. And yet, at any juncture, when you look at any shared document we have, it's incredible because there's something so powerful a force when you're an anonymous Google animal on the shared doc. And in that Google Doc, you could say a terrifying thing and it can't be traced back to you. And it's this power within the collective that prompts us. It's not trauma porn or trauma that I'm offloading, but something more along the lines of how we don't skirt away from the thing that is scary to mirror back to me. This is the diasporic experience. It's deeply powerful. You don't know who wrote it down, but you recognize truth on the page. Seeing these truths makes you feel safer to share your own truths, and you're safe because the public would never know who said what. It's a unique kind of power and beauty.

We have people who are artists, prose writers, poets, and also scholars. Everybody's got their own way of making and composing and it's so weirdly wonderful and delicious. Liberating. The collective is a safe space where nobody's trying to out-do anyone else; it's non-hierarchical and also–nobody's watching. Nobody knows what you did.

Any opportunity or invitation an individual collective member receives, generally turns into an invitation of the collective. For instance: my initiation into the collective was a situation in which I inquired and invited the collective to participate in an exhibit with me.

Someone I'd met on social media years ago was now living in Salt Lake City and curating for a small gallery there. When I was finishing up my PhD, this curator asked if I'd like to exhibit part of my dissertation. Instead of saying yes, I asked if I could invite She Who Has No Master(s) to engage in some core components of the work I'd been exploring. And the curator was enthusiastic about the idea–so then I wrote to SWHNM to see if they wanted to collaborate, and I've been a member ever since.

AC: It's a wonderful model! Working anonymously within a collective is a way of sharing power and resources. It also destabilizes hierarchies around who is more established or emerging.

DKN: A student once asked me for permission. They asked, "I was reading your book and I want to do these body image-text things. Can I do that and just write, "after Diana Khoi Nguyen?" I replied, "There's no need for the 'after'-- you can just do it, and it'll be your own thing." I mean, I definitely didn't invent concrete poetry! Nonproprietary forms! This is actually the opposite of how I feel grad school was: every writer trying to do their best at being the most unique or something. Which has some utility, but also, is really unhealthy. I had a friend who would withheld submission and contest information, not share submission deadlines, I think because she thought she had a better chance of winning if less people submitted. Which is such a scarcity mindset.

That's such a shame, because, that's not how it works. Community is vital for the writing life. It works if we all share, generate, and contribute to the hive. Every time someone wins, or succeeds, we celebrate these moments collectively. If I didn't win something, I'm just happy that someone I knew and admired won! And then I believe that I'll a little closer to being hopefully winning / receiving this opportunity (or one like it) in the future.

How to retain and nourish the spirit of generosity and good will within a collective? We have to be anti-capitalist and secretive. Doing so breeds many bad feelings and it makes it harder for one to write because one just feels shitty. And I don't want to feel shitty. I want to celebrate people, get excited, be inspired, then go home and do something explosive on the page. Then do it again and continue advocating for others in my various communities. I'm also thinking: What can I draw forth from other people, and how can I nudge people if I haven't been seeing them doing something (like writing)?

For instance, If I see someone has a proclivity or potential for trying a different genre or modality, I bring up this possibility to them. Encouragement can have surprising effects.

Sometimes I'll invite a writer to do a video with no sound (nothing fancy, just with their smart phone). And no one has asked them to do that before. So they do it, and then it leads to X, Y, and Z, and then like later down the chain of reactions, it will have like sparked a different kind of move in their short story or project. Which brings me to a vital aspect of my aesthetic, which is play. How do we get back to that early place of possibility–when we were kids in the sandbox? How to not be bogged down by doubt.

AC: Before we end our conversation I wanted to ask you about your most recent book, *Root Fractures* and how you begin with Vietnamese, a language you continue to study. I am curious about your relationship to Vietnamese and how it informs your work.

DKN: Before I answer this, I have to share a bit of context: I didn't know that Vietnamese was my first language until I watched a home video of myself as a three year old bossing everybody around, take pictures of the family in a slang-y southern Vietnamese dialect. When I started Kindergarten, my parents forbid me from speaking Vietnamese; I spoke English even when my parents spoke in Vietnamese. And then throughout my adolescence, I felt shame at not being able to speak Vietnamese around relatives.

Fast forward several years to just before the pandemic: I traveled to Saigon and began tutoring lessons with a native speaker and instructor. One of the homework questions was: Write a paragraph for your family. Immediately, I thought, "Oh, shit, I don't even know how to say all the things I need to say yet to respond to this assignment." And with my limited three weeks lessons, all I can write are elementary sentences such as, We are five, So-and-so is an architect or So-and-so is an engineer.

There's so much I don't know how to say or write–like the word for suicide.

Doing this assignment put me in this weird intersection being unable to articulate fully while feeling so much on the inside–all while trying to learn a language which I used to know. So many layers!

Season's Stranger

Madina Tuhbatullina

Summer's unbothered streetlights, bitten legs.
In this scene, it's impolite to say mother, father; to say
this is what will be and cross-legged
find your fifty-seven tales, enact them
to faces who never touched your hair
that lives in the weavings of this rug.

You haven't seen yet where my ears point
behind cheekbones: the less you retain yourself,
the more I claim you. This passing down must be prophetic.

Tacky brown curtains and mustache-less jobs
I caught through the young person's worries of older opinions.
The edema of your undereye I missed.
Love me again, not as you would a child,
but a rendition of your Sundays.
Eyebrows and landmarks that festered this gap are all
I can't tell you.

Contributor Bios & Acknowedgments

Lupita Aquino began her literary journey as a book reviewer on Instagram, quickly gaining recognition as a prominent voice in the book community. Driven by a mission to amplify Latine representation within literary spaces, she advocates for the inclusion of diverse voices across the broader literary landscape. Her dedication to connecting readers with diverse voices and books has paved the way for her to contribute book coverage to outlets such as TODAY.com, *Aster(ix) Literary Journal*, *She Reads*, *The Washington Independent Review of Books*, and more. Beyond her digital presence, Lupita is the founder of La Comunidad Reads, an author-inclusive book club in partnership with the DC Public Library. She has also moderated numerous literary events and served as a judge for the 2024 PEN/Jean Stein Book Award, the 2023 Louise Meriwether First Prize for the Feminist Press, and was a member of the Selection Committee for the 2021 Aspen Words Literary Prize. She currently serves on the Authors Committee for the Carol Shields Prize For Fiction. When not immersed in books, she enjoys exploring local bookstores and libraries with her wife and son.

Catalina Bode is a writer and educator mostly from Illinois and now lives in Ohio. Her work has been supported by a Fulbright, Tin House, the Vermont Studio Center, the Wexner Center for the Arts, the Hopwood Program, the Greater Columbus Arts Council, and as a Ricardo Salinas Scholar. She earned her MFA from the Helen Zell Writers' Program at the University of Michigan and her writing can be found in *Alaska Quarterly Review*, *The Pinch*, and *Salt Hill Journal.*

Angie Cruz is a novelist and editor. Her most recent novel *How Not To Drown in A Glass of Water* (2022) was a finalist for the 2024 Neustadt International Prize for Literature, shortlisted for The Aspen Words Literary Prize, winner of the Gold Medal, Latino Book Award/The Isabel Allende Most Inspirational Book Award, and chosen for The New York Times 100 Notable Books of 2022. Her novel, *Dominicana* was the inaugural book pick for GMA book club and shortlisted for The Women's Prize, longlisted for the Andrew Carnegie Medals for Excellence in Fiction, a RUSA Notable book and the winner of the ALA/YALSA Alex Award in fiction. Cruz is the author of two other novels, *Soledad* and *Let It Rain Coffee* and has published shorter works in *The Paris Review*, *VQR*, *Callaloo*, *Gulf Coast* and other journals. She's the co-founder and Editor-in-chief of the award-winning literary journal, *Aster(ix)*. She divides her time between Pittsburgh, New York and Turin.

Maz Do is an Indonesian-Vietnamese American writer. Her fiction has been published in print and online in *McSweeney's Quarterly Concern*, *The Baffler* and other venues. In 2023 she placed first runner-up in *McSweeney*'s inaugural Stephen Dixon prize for her short story, "When the Moths Came." She is a Kundiman Fellow, a 2022 Asian Women Writers' Mentee, a Tin House Workshop alumnus, and an MFA student in fiction at Cornell University. This year she was also granted a Fulbright Creative Arts Award for the 2024-25 academic year, which she will be spending in Yogyakarta, Indonesia.

Lauren Francis-Sharma is author of *Book of the Little Axe*, a 2020 finalist for the Hurston/Wright Award in Fiction. Her critically acclaimed first novel, *'Til the Well Runs Dry* was awarded the Honor Fiction Prize by the Black Caucus of the ALA. Lauren is a graduate of the University of Pennsylvania, the University of Michigan Law School, and the MFA Program for Writers at Warren Wilson College. Lauren serves on the board of the PEN/Faulkner Foundation and is the Assistant Director of Bread Loaf Writers' Conference. Lauren's third novel, *Casualties of Truth* will be published by Grove/Atlantic in February 2025, followed shortly by her foreword to Scribner's new edition of *Cry, the Beloved Country*.

Iliana Emilia García was born in 1970 in Santo Domingo, Dominican Republic. She is a visual artist and sculptor known for large-scale paintings and installations. She is a co-founder of the Dominican York Proyecto GRÁFICA (DYPG) Collective and lives in Brooklyn, New York.

Chioma Iwunze-Ibiam is a lecturer in Cornell University's Creative Writing program. Her literary works have received recognition from the Commonwealth Short Story Writers' Prize, the James McConkey Master of Fine Arts Creative Writing Award, the David L. Picket '84 Summer Fellowship, the Cecilia Unaegbu Prize for Fiction, the Voice of America Award for flash fiction and others. Her work has appeared in the *Mukana Press Anthology 2023*, *Ankara Press*, *Maple Tree Literary Supplement*, *Flash Fiction Press*, *Fiction 365*, *Ebedi Review Anthology*, and elsewhere. Chioma is currently working on a novel-in-stories about autism parenting and immigration.

Sangi Lama is from Hetauda, Nepal. Her writing has been supported by Kundiman, Tin House, and the Carolyn Moore Writing Residency. She is an MFA candidate in Fiction at the University of Pittsburgh.

Sandra Lee is an MFA candidate in Fiction at the University of Pittsburgh. She is working on a novel about members of a Korean American church in Queens.

Yessica Martinez is a poet from Queens, New York. Originally from Medellin, Colombia, she identifies as an illegalized person who currently holds Deferred Action for Childhood Arrivals (DACA) status. A recipient of the Amy Clampitt Residency, her poems have been published in *Los Angeles Review*, *Another Chicago Magazine*, *Interim* and *Here to Stay: Poetry and Prose from the Undocumented Diaspora*. You can follow her @yessi_poet or read her work at yessicamartinez.org

Diana Khoi Nguyen is the author of *Ghost Of* (2018) which was a finalist for the National Book Award, and *Root Fractures* (2024). Her video work has recently been exhibited at the Miller Institute for Contemporary Art. Nguyen is a Kundiman fellow and member of the Vietnamese artist collective, She Who Has No Master(s). A recipient of a fellowship from the National Endowment for the Arts, and winner of the 92Y Discovery Poetry Contest and 2019 Kate Tufts Discovery Award, she currently teaches in the Randolph College Low-Residency MFA and is an Assistant Professor at the University of Pittsburgh.

Tierney Oberhammer is a writer living in New York's Hudson Valley. Her work has appeared or is forthcoming in swamp pink, *The Adroit Journal*, *Cincinnati Review*, *Copper Nickel*, *Callaloo* and *River Teeth*. She is the recipient of support from Sewanee and the Elizabeth George Foundation. She is a member of the Wildcat Writing Group and lives with Jamie, Mariah and Wavy.

Adriana E. Ramírez is a Mexican-Colombian writer, critic, and performance poet based in Pittsburgh. She won the inaugural PEN/ Fusion Emerging Writers Prize in 2015 for her novella-length work of nonfiction, *Dead Boys* (Little A, 2016). Her reviews, essays, and poems have also appeared in *The Atlantic*, the *Los Angeles Times*, the *Boston Globe*, *ESPN's The Undefeated*, *Los Angeles Review of Books*, *Guernica/ PEN America*, and *Literary Hub* among others. She occasionally reviews books for *People Magazine*, and is a columnist and InReview editor at the *Pittsburgh Post-Gazette.* Her debut full-length work of nonfiction, The Violence, is forthcoming from Scribner.

Mauricio Ruiz is a novelist, translator, and cultural journalist. He was born in Mexico City and has lived in Norway, Belgium and the US. He's been shortlisted for the Bridport and Fish Short Story Prizes, and received fellowships from OMI Writers (New York, US), Jakob Sande (Sunnfjord, Norway), Three Seas Council (Rhodes, Greece), Société des auteurs (Brussels, Belgium), and Can Serrat (Catalonia, Spain).

His work has appeared in *Words Without Borders*, *Electric Literature*, *The Common*, *The Rumpus*, *The Masters Review*, *Letras Libres*, *Gatopardo*, among others. He has published two collections of short stories and is at work on his fourth novel. He's currently a grad student in creative writing at the University of Iowa.

Tanya Shirazi Galvez is a Los Angeles born, Lynwood raised, and Las Vegas based writer. She earned her MFA from the University of Pittsburgh and her work has appeared in Roxane Gay's *The Audacity* and *L.A. Review of Books* PubLab. She is Senior Editor of *Aster(ix) Journal* and Fiction Editor for *Witness Magazine*. She is a Black Mountain Institute PhD Fellow in Fiction at the University of Nevada, Las Vegas where she is working on her first novel.

Madina Tuhbatullina is a poet from Turkmenistan, whose work has been published or is forthcoming in *The Indianapolis Review*, *Spoon River Poetry Review*, *Tar River Poetry* and elsewhere. Her poetry collection Tender Knots was named a finalist for the Black Lawrence Press Immigrant Writing Series. Madina is a Creative Writing MFA candidate at the University of Nevada, Las Vegas and a Managing Editor at *Interim*.

Alexandra Watson is a multiracial fiction writer and poet from Syracuse, New York. She's the executive editor of *Apogee Journal*, which won the 2022 Whiting Literary Magazine Prize, and for which she received the 2019 PEN/Nora Magid Prize for Literary Magazine editing and the 2023 Platinum Review Award for magazine editing from the Council of Literary Magazines and Presses. Her poetry and fiction have appeared in *The Nation*, *The South Carolina Review*, *The Rumpus*, *Bennington Review*, *The Common*, *Nat. Brut.*, *The Offing*, *Cake Zine*, and others. She's a Senior Lecturer at Barnard College, where she founded the Creative Writing Fellows program and the Cite Black Barnard Faculty initiative. She lives in the Hudson Valley.

www.ingramcontent.com/pod-product-compliance
Lightning Source LLC
Chambersburg PA
CBHW032010180726
48283CB00008B/2606

* 9 7 8 1 9 4 2 5 4 7 2 3 5 *